Enneagram For Business

The Power of the Enneagram and the Sacred
Enneagram

(Understanding Love and Relationship With a
Practical Approach)

Armando Neal

Published by Knowledge Icons

Armando Neal

Enneagram For Business: The Power of the Enneagram and the Sacred Enneagram (Understanding Love and Relationship With a Practical Approach)

ISBN 978-1-990084-50-8

Legal & Disclaimer

suggested remedies, techniques, or information in this book.

Upon using the information contained in this book, you agree to hold harmless the Author from and against any damages, costs, and expenses, including any legal fees potentially resulting from the application of any of the information provided by this guide. This disclaimer applies to any damages or injury caused by the use and application, whether directly or indirectly, of any advice or information presented, whether for breach of contract, tort, negligence, personal injury, criminal intent, or under any other cause of action.

You agree to accept all risks of using the information presented inside this book. You need to consult a professional medical practitioner in order to ensure you are both able and healthy enough to participate in this program.

Table of Contents

Introduction

This book contains proven steps and strategies on how to understand and make the most of your Enneagram personality type. When you understand your Enneatype, and the Types of those around you, you begin to unlock the secrets of your potential. You can build better relationships, experience more happiness, and increase your overall wellness. This powerful tool of human psychology can put you in touch with your feelings and natural inclinations, making it easy for you to "live your best life."

In this book, you'll discover some of the driving forces behind people's actions. You'll gain insight into not only who people are, but why they are who they are, and you'll find practical suggestions on how to recognize when someone is under stress, then help them be their best. And when I say "someone", I also mean you! Your self-care is essential, and this book aims to help you make it easy to care for yourself, no matter what your personal goals, background, or Ennea-type.

The simple, everyday concepts and suggestions to help you manage stress, enhance your relationships, and learn from your struggles are things you can begin doing immediately, at your own pace, and in the way that works for you. Flexible and adaptable, yet proven, the Enneagram assists millions around the world every day, and I've put together this book to make it easy for you to use it, too.

Thanks again for purchasing this book. I hope you enjoy it!

Chapter1:

Theenneagramasaframeworkforundersta nding Themultidimensional Nature Of Personality

The Enneagram is contrary to what so many people think they know about personality. It is a far more liberating take.

It's true that just like other personality typology systems, it specifies various categories, that's not all there is to it. The enneagram of personality operates on the principle that human beings, by nature, are complex and therefore cannot be put into little tidy boxes. The Enneagram takes into account the many aspects of a human being's personality, and his free will – his capacity to make decisions and show behavior based on who he is and what he feels in right, or what he feels he needs.

In this chapter, we will put the Enneagram under the proverbial microscope. In addition, in order to give you an in-depth understanding of this system as a psychometry tool, we will take a close look at the science of personality.

What is The Enneagram?

The Enneagram of Personality is a personality typing and development system that makes use ofa diagram to plot ideas that philosophers have been developing for centuries.

Enneagram is derived from the Greek words Enne which means Nine, and Gramma, which alludes to something "written" or "drawn". It translates to "Nine Points" – and that is what an Enneagram diagram looks like -- an image of a circle with three clusters representing the three centers of intelligence and with each one having 3 points. This amounts to 9 points that represent a certain personality archetype with the numbers arranged clockwise as in the following image.

When you take a look at the modern enneagram, you would notice that it's pretty straightforward and easier to comprehend. Man operates according to basic fears and desires, which may also vary depending on which center of his being is more dominant

This is in fact the product of years of development by the Enneagram community. They were, however, firmly rooted in Oscar Ichazo's theories on ego-types.

The 9 Archetypes

The 21st century Enneagram of Personality is known to feature the Nine personality archetypes. Keep in mind that the following are just an overview and do not depict the full spectrum of an archetype's personality.

Type 1 – The Discerning, Principled, Well-organized, Self-Controlled, and Perfectionistic Reformer

Type 2 – The generous, warm-hearted, sincere, self-sacrificing , and possessive Helper

Type 3 – The flexible,driven, competent, ambitious, and image-conscious Achiever

Type 4 – The expressive, sensitive, self-aware, temperamental, and self-absorbed Individualist

Type 5 – The innovative, insightful, curious, alert, and isolatedInvestigator

Type 6 – The reliable, hardworking, engaging, anxious, and defensiveLoyalist

Type 7 – The vivacious, spontaneous, versatile, adventurous,and scattered Enthusiast

Type 8 – The assertive, self-confident, willful, domineeringand confrontational Challenger

Type 9 – The receptive, supportive, reassuring, accepting, and complacent Peacemaker

The Enneagram has been partially validated in empirical and experiential studies, as published in Anna Suttons 2012 review "But is it real?" A review of research on the Enneagram." published on the Enneagram journal. Its proponents have done remarkable work in the subject of psychology, such as Dr. David Daniels who was a clinic professor of psychiatry at Stanford University Medical School.

Enneagram teachers and advocates have also drawn from the work of psychologists such as that of Karen Horney, a German psychoanalyst, in order to develop their own Enneagram theories.

Beyond The Surface: Personality Theories

Before you delve into the complex world of integration and the Enneagram, it's important to have an understanding of personality, particularly personality development.

What Exactly is integration?

The enneagram is used with integration as the ultimate goal. Integration is the goal of personality analysis that drove humans into learning the enneagram in the first place.

It refers is the state of being in which all aspects of your personality are in harmony. Experiencing integration means knowing full well who you are, accepting it, and making use of your strengths and weaknesses in order to be the best you can be – not the best person in the world but the best you and only you can possibly be.

It entails exploring what you truly are even though you might not like what you find.

In a way, integration is one of the ways in which you can achieve self-actualization. It's brought by the desire to be fulfilled and be fully alive, whatever it may mean to a person. And it requires vulnerability because it requires you to accept all aspects of yourself including those that lie way beyond the surface – things that introspection and analysis could help uncover.

Personality 101

'Personality' is such a ubiquitous word but you'd be surprised to know that as of writing, there is no universal definition. What most experts and personality theorists agree on is that a pattern of behavior, traits and attitudes that give both a consistency and a unique to a certain person.

Personality Development, therefore, is the process in which all these things develop which ultimately shaped a person into everything that he is – and into his own person. This can include so many things that have yet to be studied closely including a person's temperament, culture, experiences, and environment. It could also refer to your own efforts to understand yourself and improve your behavior or how you interact with the world.

The consensus of the scientific community is that when it comes to personality, there are two key concepts to keep in mind – traits and mechanisms.

Traits - Let's focus on this one word that we'll be encountering throughout this book. It's the center of personality psychology.

Traits are an aspect of personality which are known toinfluence behavior. The key word here is influence. It does not dictate your behavior outright.

Human beings are adaptable. In addition, everyone is unique by default and everyone is also shaped by their own unique environment and experiences.

Nonetheless, it cannot be denied that traits do affect behavior. For example, someone who is egocentric will likely lash out if his authority is questioned.

However, even though we tend to react in a specific way most of the time, there's no guarantee that we will react that way all the time. For example, even if you are generally an amiable person, you are amiable, this doesn't mean that you never lose your cool or lash out. Those who are good-natured, can still have days in which they 'act out of character' and this can happen for so many reasons – they might be having a bad day, they might be worried about something, or they're irritable because you've been up all night. It's not cut and dried.

Mechanisms - Now that we've highlighted how crucial traits are as a component of personality, it's also important to understand how personality works -- its mechanisms.

People may exhibit behavior depending on their traits and their decision rules

Here's the personality process visualized:

Input -> Decision Rules -> Output

Input refers to the thing sin your environment that you need to react. Decision rules, in the context of psychology, refer to the rules you set that indicate how you're going to choose between multiple outcomes.

For example, you're a typically punctual person. You are supposed to go to a meeting the next day (an input) but you're extremely tired after a long day and there are only a few hours left before daytime (another input). This can go multiple ways:

1) You can sleep in and apologize when you arrive late.

2) You can try to reschedule well ahead of time.

3) You can set your alarm clock and wake up early despite feeling like a zombie.

If one of your traits is punctuality, and your motivation is success in your career and maintaining competence, you will likely exhibit behavior #3.That behavior is the output of your traits as well as the personality mechanisms at work.

This is just an illustration. In reality, human beings are so complex. Even if you are not the punctual kind, if you believe that your career trumps all, then you'll still show up on time. Also, if you are the punctual type but you also believe in self-care and knowing exactly what you're capable of (or incapable of when you lack sleep), you might end up going for Option #2 and negotiating for another schedule.

You will see these traits and mechanisms in action as we go through the individual sections for each character type of the Enneagram.

Freud's Three Aspects of Personality

To have more context on personality analysis, it helps to take a look at the theories that psychoanalysts have developed in an attempt to understand man and the inner workings of the human mind.

Freud is a proponent of the theory that the human psyche – the totally of your mind including your conscious and subconscious mind -- is structured into three parts. These are the id, the ego, and the superego, and each of them develops at a certain stage in our life. Note that these are systems that operate from your brain and they are in no way physical.

The Id is the primitive part of our mind. It's what drives our base desires. It involves our aggressive and sexual drives.

The id is impulsive and operates purely on the pleasure principle. It's constantly chasing after what it desires. Perhaps the best example of the id manifesting itself is when a baby cries for food. The id doesn't concern itself with looking desperate – it just needs to be satisfied. The id actually remains infantile throughout our entire lives.

The ego is that part of us which develops in order to mediate between the id and the superego while keeping the external world as part of the equation. It's the part of you that drives decision making.

While the id is chaotic and irrational as it purely operates on pleasure, the ego operates on reason. Or at least, that's what a healthy ego should do. It operates on reality in order to come up with a reasonable way to come up with the id's demands, which typically entails delaying gratification. It takes society's rules into account while still chasing pleasure.

The superego, on the other hand, contains all the values and morals that we learned from society and from our environment (such as our parents and teachers) as we grow up and get exposed to the world. It usually develops around ages 3 to 5. It's function is to rein in the impulses of the id, particularly those that society deems as taboo, such as sex and aggression.

It has two components – the ideal self, and the conscience. The conscience punishes the ego to reinforce the idea that something should not or should be done; this is done through feelings of guilt. The ideal self is a person's notion of what he should be in order to be proud of himself. The conscience and ideal self are developed depending on how you were brought up so parental values may play a role.

Each aspect of personality has its unique features and systems of dealing with the external world. However, they all interact in order to form the essence of our being. All three of them contributes to our behavior.

As you take a look at the Nine Archetypes of the Enneagram of personality and how each of them operates, you would notice that the Id is at constantly at work, and so are the ego and the superego.

Depth Psychology Theory

A person's mind is made up of the conscious and the unconscious.

The conscious mind is where you are aware of who you are (or at least, who you think you are) and your existence. It's the part that processes what you perceive, feel, or think. It's where the ego resides.

Some psychologists believe that psychological problems can occur when there's a problem with your unconscious mind, and it can manifest in your behavior and personality formation.

The unconscious mind contains all the things that you are not aware of and the things that you cannot always access directly or at will. This includes things such as mental processes, motivations, and memory. Carl Jung even has a theory in which the unconscious mind has 2 layers – the personal unconscious and the collective unconsciousness. The first one is the collection of things you encountered or knew at one point but cannot recall. The collective unconscious refers to all the things that human beings as a specie have developed over time, such as certain fears of something, or thumb sucking for comfort. These two likely play a role with what people call "instinct" today.

Freud took it further by suggesting that there are three levels as opposed to two –

the conscious, subconscious, and unconscious. The subconscious refers to easily accessible memories, usually recent. He theorized that it filters the information you receive and then validates that information based on your own value system.

It cannot be denied that despite the many wise men who have attempted to uncover the mysteries of the human psyche, we are still pretty much in the dark. However, integration just may be possible if we can use the enneagram as a map to navigate this mostly uncharted theory

The Precursor: Ichazo's Enneagrams

The personality types in the modern Enneagram were derived primarily from Oscar Ichazo's theories on ego-types. Here, we'll take a look at how Ichazo used the Enneagram to map out what he called ego types which involve fixations, holy ideas, traps, passion and virtues. Note that while these may have some allusions to religion and can be used in the context of faith-based teachings, the Enneagram is actually a handy psychometry tool that can be used even without that aspect.

It can instead be used as a tool for gaining enlightenment – the awakening of your true nature.Note that this is going to be a reader's digest version of Ichazo' teachings designed to anchor the philosophy behind the Nine types. We encourage you to seek them out and learn more.

Fixations

Fixations refer to the persistent focus of the id. It's what the id is constantly chasing after. They typically occur when an issue or conflict occurs during a child's developmental stage. Some fixations are obvious – some people tend to engage in smoking, eating or nail biting when stressed and they're said to have oral fixations.However, they actually manifest as habits. It's what your mind tends to go to even when you don't direct it, and from a subconscious level, it affects how you deal with the outside world.In this

Enneagram, Ichazo plotted the nine ways in which a person can become fixated.

Enneagram of Fixations

One of these fixations tends to be dominate in a person. Each of the 9 fixations is labelled to indicate the archetype it is associated with. For example, the fixation for most type 9s is indolence.

Holy Ideas

According to Ichazo, fixations can be remedied by a holy idea – the one thing that provides clarity. The Holy Idea is the product of the realization that there's something greater than ourselves. It's what the ego lost when it erected a wall between the self and the outside world. For example, The fixation Stinginess can be remedied by Omniscience. When someone uses a Holy Idea to deal with a fixation, he will get a direct and authentic perception of reality.

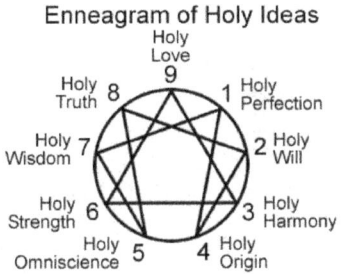

Enneagram of Holy Ideas

Traps

Traps masquerade as remedies. Sometimes, we might think that something is the solution to a fixation, and that solution turns out to have only made things worse – that's a trap. For example, the Type 9 trap – Seeker does not really remedy the fixation of Indolence. In fact, it reinforces it. You'll notice that the Trap and Holy Idea for Type 1 is the same — perfection. However, whereas Holy Perfection refers to authentic perfection, the Trap perfection refers to the ego's own sense of perfection and its attempts to shape the world according to its own distorted interpretation.

Enneagram of Traps

Passions

Passions refer to the 'energy' that feed a person's fixation. For example, a person's misguided pursuit of a Trap — Security — can be driven by fear. Fear can push a person toward creating an environment or inserting himself in an environment that he deems safer.

Enneagram of Passions

Laziness
9
Excess 8   1 Anger
Gluttony 7   2 Pride
Fear 6   3 Deceit
Avarice 5   4 Envy

Virtues

A problem can occur when passion gets in the way of virtue. Sometimes, we become caught up in fixations and traps that we end up losing touch with the right way to do things. We can find virtue by managing if not eliminating passions in the context of the Enneagram. For example, the Type 1 virtue is serenity. A person caught up in resentment in his quest for perfection can find freedom from the fixation and reduce feelings of anger, thereby finding serenity.

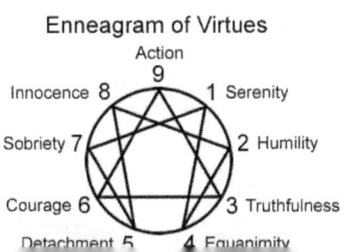

Enneagram of Virtues

Action
9
Innocence 8   1 Serenity
Sobriety 7   2 Humility
Courage 6   3 Truthfulness
Detachment 5   4 Equanimity

For a more detailed analysis of the enneagram and its inner workings, we suggest studying Ichazo's theories. This book is meant to focus on the nine personality archetypes of the modern enneagram with the goal of helping you determine your type.

Chapter 2: The Enneagram Theory For

Development

The Enneagram philosophy, as it applies to the growth of ourselves first, is one of exploratory where we are at the instant in the nine-point scheme. It also takes a look at which points we go to when in times of stress, or those types of bad ways or impacts we permit to disturb us when we are in an unhealthy state. Diagonally, the system also takes a look at where we go to in times of security or the types of good behaviors or effects that we let to affect us when we are in a improved state of life.

It is a solid tool for self-awareness and self-knowledge. But as with anything that causes us to turn inner, the work needing to be done to heal ourselves and bring us to a advanced state of being can be very difficult, and sometimes even aching. This is not a concept that tags you and then forever sticks you with that tag. The

Enneagram helps to open new paths and procedures to advanced learning and consciousness. It is not about sticking you in a single region, but rather, it teaches you to get "unstuck" from wherever or whichever point you may presently find yourself within.

The Enneagram is authorizing, teaching you how to know how and why you respond to certain circumstances and people in the way that you do, and then to take accountability for your actions and actions and change them into something far more influential to aid you move through life, and to stop hurting not only others, but to stop hurting yourself in the procedure.

We are all individuals. We act and react in certain behaviors. We are all legal individuals with rationality to the way we feel. However, we all have knowledgeable life and bad things, and even helpful things have wedged and maybe even contaminated the way we reply to the world around us. It is time to take a serious look at ourselves if we truly want to expand into the final shared awareness.

The Enneagram is about discovering your true self and learning how to pardon that personality to raise. Each step on the trip is one of finding and vision into who you are and who those around you are as well. The Enneagram teaches us not only that we respond to procedures, but that in realism, we are responding to our *insight* of those. How we observe what occurs around us is founded on our perplexing through those things that have happened in the ancient, and conveying a hypothesis founded on where we are in that insight. We come to learn that awareness is not always authentic. All too often, reality and our perception of it are not even close. By learning the how and why we do perceive things, and react like this to them, we can come closer to reality, which brings us closer to the shared awareness and eventually, closer to the Godly.

Understanding ourselves through the Enneagram is not only about realizing the decent side characteristic in our nature founded on where we are at on our individual expeditions, but also learning the evil sides, the dark within us. It is only by noticing these features of self that we can eventually renovate and heal ourselves, our lives, and the world around us.

The foundation of the Enneagram starts with the evidence that we grow our character type based on actions that have formed who we have become from the integral issues attributed to us even before our time of birth, through childhood and youth, up to our present-day selves. But this is only the start, defining the idea of our "Basic Self." What we do with that self is up to us. Our Basic Self also varies through diverse parts based on fit and unhealthy life points and skills and can climb up and down the developing ladder within each Enneatype. This simple ladder can take us through the phases of growth in our lives from unhealthy features, through regular parts of self, all the way up through the higher, healthier heights that are the perfect to attain.

There are no "good" or "bad" personality types. They all have ideals within them that may be more attractive at one point in your life or another, or that society may favor, founded on where we are at in our social growth. Every Enneatype has a drive and a variety of unhealthy to healthy behavior characters and the way we reply to circumstances. Not all Enneatypes may reply to conditions in the same way.

Take the time to realize who you are, founded on the Enneagram, and use the knowledges within to improve yourself, your life, your relationships to others, and your relationship to the world around you. There is no right or wrong way. There are no rulings. There is only doing the work as you see needed, self-determining of what others think or trust. The Enneagram is about you... and eventually your linking to the Heavenly and to the divine nature within.

Chapter 3: The Difference Between

People With High And Low Ei

We have defined emotional intelligence as the ability to recognize, understand, and manage emotions. This extends to the ability to recognize and influence the emotions of others around us. The level of awareness of our own emotions drive how we behave and eventually affect people, whether positively or negatively.

In our endless attempts at understanding those who we interact with, viewing someone from the EI perspective makes getting to know them easier. How do you tell if a person has high EI? What are the indications of low EI in a person?

Low emotional intelligence negatively impacts most, if not all, areas of any person's life. There will often be a certain awkwardness in school, work, family, friendships, even in romantic relationships. A lot of a low EI person's relationships will often feel strained or problematic.

An emotionally intelligent person is keenly in touch with his emotions, including frustration, sadness, and all else unpleasant. He or she has no difficulty identifying the emotion, thus managing it is nearly effortless as well. People with high EI are just as in tune to the emotions of others. This sensitivity to emotions, both of the self and of others, renders these people as better partners, friends, parents, and leaders.

If you think that your emotional skills could use a little work, or if you believe you have the makings of a healthy EI, the good news is that these abilities can be assimilated and, yes... enhanced.

Below are a few more specific characteristics of individuals with high EI:

You ponder on feelings. The first indicator of emotional intelligence is awareness — both of the self and of the society in which you belong. With this, you are able to recognize emotions and their impact on yourself and on others. This kind of awareness stems from frequent reflection. You ask yourself questions like:

What are my strengths, emotionally? Where am I weakest?

In what ways do my moods affect my thoughts and decisions?

What might be going on beneath the surface causing (another person) to behave that way?

Reflecting on questions like these puts you at an advantage in regulating your behavior and influencing others' as well.

You appreciate the "power" of the pause. You have no trouble taking a thoughtful moment before you speak or act, especially in complicated or charged situations. You know how important it is to calculate your moves in order to avoid embarrassing moments or making commitments hastily. Simply put, pausing helps you avoid making irreversible decisions based on momentary emotions.

You take criticism constructively. Typically, people dread negative feedback. But you believe that criticism is a valuable learning opportunity. And even when criticism appears baseless, you still accept this as a helpful preview to how others might perceive you. For you, criticism always brings you to ask yourself: "How can this help me be better?"

You operate with genuineness or sincerity. Sincerity is not necessarily about always sharing everything about you to everyone. This genuineness is about staying loyal to your values and principles, saying what you mean, and meaning what you say. It's true, not everyone will welcome what you have to say. What's important is that you are true and the ones who actually matter will appreciate you more for it.

You are empathic. You are connected with others through thoughts and feelings. You do not judge or label people; instead, you try to view things from their perspective. You understand that empathy does not mean that you agree with another person's point of view. Empathy is about your natural willingness to understand their position.

You are quick to praise. It is human nature to crave recognition or appreciation. You are always focused on the good in others. When you are generous with sincere praises, this helps build trust that you are an objective, selfless individual. This inspires others to work harder and always aim to reach their full potential.

You are able to give meaningful feedback. You are perfectly able to frame criticism as constructive feedback. This is because you know that criticism comes with the possibility of being offensive to some. You always strive to be helpful rather than harmful.

You apologize. You possess the humility that gives you courage to easily seek forgiveness whenever you know that you've committed errors. This humility will allow others to trust you better. An emotionally intelligent person believes that apologizing is more about valuing relationships above one's own self-esteem.

You are forgiving. You have fully realized that holding on to resentment is like leaving a bullet inside a gunshot wound, preventing any kind of absolute healing. While he or she who has offended you may have moved on with his or her life, harboring resentment is like denying yourself the opportunity to fully heal. When you forgive, you let go of residual hurt and free yourself from any form of emotional hold by those who do not deserve it. You know that this is the only way to move forward.

You keep your promises. Nowadays, it is easy for a lot of people to just skip on commitments for, sometimes, the flimsiest of reasons. An emotionally intelligent person has made a habit of keeping his word. In things both big and small, you endeavor to keep your promises. This proves to everyone that you are reliable and trustworthy.

You are altruistic. You possess a genuine selfless concern for others. The best way to make a positive impact on others is to help them. You know that a person's real worth is not measured by his college degrees or career accomplishments. What turns you into a true person of substance has more to do with the amount of time he you devote to helping others. Being sincerely altruistic influences others to trust you and follow your generous lead.

You defend yourself against emotional sabotage. So, yes, emotional intelligence is the ability to recognize and manage the emotions of others as well as your own. Herein lies the dark side of EI: some people might attempt to manipulate others to their detriment for some selfish cause. And this is one of the reasons why you continue to exercise your own emotional intelligence: it is so you can protect yourself from self-serving attempts like these from others.

On the other end of the spectrum, you can detect a person with low EI if he or she is:

Frequently getting into arguments. Individuals with low EI are somehow challenged in their understanding of the emotions of others and this difficulty often finds them getting into arguments. People with opportunities for emotional intelligence seem to easily get embroiled in heated disagreements with friends, family, co-workers, and even random strangers. Their inability to manage their emotions well together with a disconnect from other people's emotions cause them to instinctively construe disagreement as heated conflict.

Unable to interpret how others feel. Low EI individuals are typically oblivious (or "dense", in popular speak) to other people's feelings. They do not seem to "get" when other people are angry with or dislike them. Worse, people with low EI would always resent why others seem to expect him or her to know how they are feeling. Emotions, in general, can be quite exasperating for low EI individuals.

Unable to cope with highly emotional situations. Related to the previous characteristic, the exasperation over emotions that low EI individuals feel results to an inability to cope with strong emotions. In other words, emotions, both their own or others', are hard to understand, much less deal with. A low EI individual would typically just walk away from highly emotional situations. Concealing their true feelings is also typical for low EI individuals.

Quick to dismiss other people as "too sensitive". People with low EI seem to perceive emotional signals inaccurately. This is why it may be typical for them to be cracking jokes at the most inopportune times. And when the other people around convey a certain annoyance or dislike for these inappropriate jokes or comments, the low EI individual would always dismiss them as simply being overly sensitive.

Lacks empathy. It then comes as no surprise that someone with an inability to understand other people's emotions would have little to no empathy for others. It would, of course, be impossible for a low EI individual to "put himself in another person's shoes" since he does not get what that other person is feeling to begin with.

Close-minded to other points of view. To a low EI person, he or she is always right. They will always vigorously defend their position and refuse to consider what other people have to say, especially if it negates their own views. A low EI person is often pessimistic and hyper-critical of other people's emotions.

Quick to blame others for mistakes. When things go wrong, people with low EI would instinctively blame others. They would typically attribute the error of their own actions to the conditions of the situation or to the behavior of others, other than owning up to it. To their mind, they were forced into error by external factors and all the others are just not understanding their situation. This refusal to take responsibility thus often leaves them feeling bitter or victimized.

Prone to emotional outbursts. A low EI person's inability to understand and manage his or her emotions render him or her prone to unexpected emotional outbursts. These outbursts would typically be uncontrollable or overwrought.

Has difficulty keeping friendships. At the end of the day, with all this awkwardness in social situations earlier described, low EI individuals will show a difficulty in maintaining friendships. Deep and meaningful friendships require a "give-and-take" dynamic when it comes to feelings, compassion, and support. All these would be a struggle for someone with low EI.

Chapter 4: Enneagram Type 8 - The Confronter/Boss

The Challenger is a nickname used to describe the Enneatype 8, one of the nine types in the Enneagram.

Defining Characteristics of the Enneagram Type 8

Independent and self-sufficient

Fierce and certain look

Determination and stamina

Very energetic and busy

Fiery passions and power

Stubborn and headstrong

Serious about control over environment

Not sure if you're an Enneagram Type 8? Take our free Enneagram test.

What are Challengers like?

Goal-oriented and self-competent, challengers trail blaze boldly through all walks of life and take great pride in their independence and sharp minds. They hold their heads up high and will pick themselves right back up after each stumble—stronger than before. As children, they may have been called 'bossy' by peers. They typically take charge during group projects or meetings and find themselves at ease in leadership positions. The opinions of others will have absolutely no effect on their standings upon an issue, as they pride themselves on being fully capable and self-sufficient.

What are the Challenger's core values?

Competence, influence, power and control—Challengers crave respect as opposed to status or being liked by the group. Challengers are set to make an impact, and won't back down. They pride themselves on their strength, honesty and the truth. Challengers also possess an extremely strong inner sense of justice. Loyalty also plays a major role in Challengers' value system. They're devoted to those who have proven themselves over time and will stand by them until the end—through hell and high water. When danger comes and their loved ones are in trouble, the Challenger will confidently stretch their wings to protect them.

How can I recognize a Type 8?

Naturally accustomed to leadership roles, the Challenger makes their presence known and carries an aura of confidence and self-assuredness in their speech and walk. They typically believe in the mantra of creating your own luck and work very hard to make things happen, no questions asked. Challengers are ruthlessly independent are unafraid of confrontation, which can get them into major trouble at times. They naturally butt heads with authority, especially when met with the classic, "You must do this, because I told you so." Respect is earned through reason and competency, and not through age or status.

What are Challengers like under different levels of health?

At healthy levels: Challengers can be a champion of ideas for those who are oppressed. They're strong and confident leaders who can be the backbone and driving force for causes and communities. Their energy and commitment to improve upon society and themselves blossoms into new gardens where Challengers can sow their seeds with care. To close friends and family members, Challengers are generous and intensely loving individuals who freely offer refuge and advice. When they learn to develop their caring side, gratitude and joy emerges from their core selves. With this newfound sense of tenderness, Challengers become aware of others' needs and will freely drop the 'tough' persona.

At average levels: Challengers are competitive and may view friendships or business relations as a battlefield, always looking for the next challenge to win.

They're assertive and stubborn, but also self-confident and competent. During their down time, they critically evaluate their actions and work towards self-improvement. They avoid showing vulnerability, which can be a roadblock for connection and intimacy. Doing so would demonstrate weakness, which is absolutely unacceptable in their books. As a result, they can be seen as highly ambitious yet intimidating by peers. Their confidence and stamina lifts them to new heights, with each failure serving as a kick for more effort.

At unhealthy levels: Challengers can become tyrannical and intimidating, scaring others off at first glance. They become addicted to the pursuit of power, and will destroy anything blocking their way with fury. The feelings and emotions of others become insignificant, as they become blindfolded to the softer side of the human psyche. When their delusions of power get out of hand, Challengers become stone-cold and take an antagonistic stand to anyone who dares to question them and their motives. They may use empty threats to regain power over others and turn existing relationships into tests—where one can only pass or fail. Others may turn their backs on Challengers, who will reason that they were better off working alone. In the end, they may force themselves into loneliness.

Big on authenticity - they tend to call a spade a spade- and perhaps, as a consequence, somewhat low on empathy, types 8 tend to thrive on challenge and are prepared to deal with just about anything that life has to offer. They see themselves as the "knights" of the kingdom and their job is to protect the innocent and the less able.

Their underlying motivation is a feeling of weakness so to avoid this, types 8 develop a heightened sense of power. You can feel their presence as soon as they enter a room. These personality types thrive in the military or political world. From a positive viewpoint, their personality make up means that they are extremely resourceful and will always stand up for those they view to be less able. They also encourage others to have more belief in themselves and to stand firm in their convictions.

They tend to believe that the end justifies the means so manipulate situations to their advantage. They tend to see situations in a black and white way which can cause them to be inflexible. Their underlying desire is for power, not prestige, which can lead to bullying. They have the innate ability to spot a weakness in their opponents. They may not always win the battle, but if you take them on, you will know you have been in a fight.

Do you think you may fit the role of the Confronter/Boss?

Do you often find yourself fighting for other people's rights with no fear of any repercussions?

Do people who take ages to make a point irritate you the most?

Are you a natural leader?

Do you think you are a practical person i.e. the one to get the job done?

Some tips to help make the positive side of your personality type shine through:

Learn to control your "confrontational" side.

Life is not black and white. Human beings create complex problems and it may not always be apparent which side is the "right" one.

Learn to allow others to take the lead sometimes.

Learn to manage your anger properly. Suppressing your angry feelings isn't enough as that can cause problems too.

Work on your tendency to bully and be controlling. Concentrate on remembering that everyone is not created equal - some are not as strong as others and it is these

people that need your protection not
you're bullying.

Chapter 5: The Achiever (Type 3)

Also known as the Performer

Fifteen Signs You're an Achiever

You like to get things done and are more than willing to work hard to achieve your goals.

You can find it hard to slow down and you might struggle to find time to relax.

Patience is not one of your virtues!

Those around you describe you as a "Type A" personality.

You tend to store tension in your chest and heart area.

You have no problem setting aside your hobbies to chase success in your primary goal.

You love a challenge and relish throwing everything you have into meeting that challenge.

If at first you don't succeed, you will try, try, try again.

Your biggest fear is failure and this can cause you much stress and anxiety.

You focus on appearance. You can become overly concerned with your image and how other people perceive you.

A question you are often asked is, "How do you achieve so much?"

You very much enjoy a sense of completion and accomplishment. There's nothing like ticking boxes off your to-do list!

You are highly competitive and this is something that drives you.

You are 'self-made' in some way, having got to where you are in life by hard work and determined pursuit of your goals.

You have a lot of energy and others might describe you as having a zest for life which they often find attractive.

What do you think? Have many of the above points resonated with you?

The Achiever: An Overview

As the name suggests, the Type Three on the Enneagram is all about success. It is of vital importance to this type that their success is acknowledged. The Achiever requires this validation in order to feel worthy. They are highly focused, hard-working and competitive. These goals are often in the business world but they are not restricted to this sphere by any means. The Three is commonly a 'self-made' success, often skilled in the art of networking. Generally extroverted, the Achiever can sometimes be charismatic. There is a boundless energy and plenty of drive. Their shadow side is their secret fear of failure.

The Achiever, or the Performer, is frequently image-conscious and as such, can be slow to let his or her real self be shown. This can make intimacy difficult. The Three fears others getting too close lest they discover what they are really like.

Because of the Type Three's strong requirement for external validation, they sometimes make the error of chasing external success while ignoring their deeper needs and desires. The Achiever needs to guard against falling in to such a trap.

Notable Three's from the worlds of history, politics, sports and the arts include Bill Clinton, Arnold Schwarzenegger, Oprah Winfrey, Madonna, Lady Gaga, Will Smith, Augustus Caesar, Tony Blair, Andy Warhol, Elvis Presley, Barbra Streisand, Richard Gere, Reese Witherspoon, Anne Hathaway, Justin Bieber, Jon Bon Jovi, Paul McCartney, Lance Armstrong, O.J,Simpson, Truman Capote, Muhammad Ali, Emperor Constantine, Prince William, Carl Lewis, Tony Robbins, Deepack Chopra, Michael Jordan, Sting, Brooke Shields, Tiger Woods, Taylor Swift, Tom Cruise, Demi Moore, Courtney Cox and Kevin Spacey.

The Achiever Levels

Healthy

Authenticity

So genuine and appealing, the Three at their best is literally dripping with gentleness and benevolence. They have learned to fully accept themselves and to listen to their own internal guidance systems. These Threes are everything they appear to be as they have come to understand that they have nothing to hide. They are modest when it comes to their innate strengths and achievements and they are typically big-hearted people with a delightfully self-deprecating humour.

Competence

The high self-esteem of a healthy Three assists them in believing in themselves and their own capabilities. This type is self-assured with plenty of energy to get the job done and get it right. There is an intrinsic self-belief and a deep awareness of their own value as human beings. They are competent and confident enough to adapt to all sorts of situations and remain gracious and charming in the process.

Many people will be naturally drawn to a healthy Three.

Ambitious

These Threes are ambitious in the very best sense of the word. Never ruthless, just eager to be the best version of themselves and to fulfill their potential. Self-improvement is a driving force for these people. The healthy Achiever has it in him or her to become an outstanding human, possessing a tremendous amount of admirable qualities. Other people tend to admire them greatly and try to emulate them. This makes the healthy Three a master motivator.

Neutral

Driven

The average Type Three sets great store in doing their job well. Unfortunately, at this level, their motivation for this can be slightly less healthy and based more frequently on an abject terror of failure. They worry very much about what other people think of them and base their self-worth on the achievement of goals. It is said that comparison is the thief of joy. It certainly is for this type. This less than healthy Three will compare his or herself with others in a quest for their own status and self-worth. This is the level of the social climber or the one who believes that a career is everything.

Image-Consciousness

The Achiever can care far too much about how he or she is perceived by others. This can cause them to be "phony" in some ways as they try to conform with the real or imagined expectations of others. They can certainly excel in practicality and efficiency but they risk losing touch with their feelings in their desire to impress. This can lead to issues with intimacy.

Self-Promotion

The intense desire to impress others can cause the Three, at this level of maturity, to promote themselves ceaselessly and aggressively. They might elevate their achievements to this cause. It might feel a little like the childish tendency to say "look at me!" Inflated notions of themselves may arise and they may come across as arrogant and full of contempt, but this is just an attempt to disguise their jealousy.

Unhealthy

Fear of Failure

The Achiever at this level is willing to do or say whatever they consider necessary to preserve their image. Fear of failure and humiliation is intense at this point and can lead them to exploitative and opportunistic behaviours. They will be extremely jealous of another person's success and will strive to preserve their fragile illusion of superiority at all costs.

Deception

These folks can become so terrified at the thought of their mistakes and misdeeds being exposed that they will resort to all sorts of devious behaviours to cover up such failings. This means, of course, that the Achiever at this unhealthy level can absolutely not be trusted. They might betray or sabotage somebody just to get one up on them and their jealous states can border on delusional.

Narcissism

This is the Three at their absolute worst, when their actions correspond with the description of the Narcissistic Personality Disorder. They will stop at nothing to ruin another person's happiness and their destructiveness can become obsessive. The vindictiveness of the profoundly unhealthy Three can border on the psychopathic.

The Achiever Wings

Type Three with a Two Wing (3W2)

When you envisage the "typical" salesperson, you might well be picturing the Type Three with a Two wing. The Achiever's desire to be admired overtakes the Type Two's desire to please others and make them feel good. Although, if it's possible, they may well do both. This variety of the number Three is usually extroverted and can come across as attractive and even seductive. Their persona is cheerful and calm and they will be keen to show their best side and want to be perceived as having it together emotionally.

The influence of the Two wing on the Three personality, can make their "shine" more genuine. At best, this variety of the Three is big on self-observation and likely to be a humble type. They'll also be friendly and likeable with great social skills that cause others to enjoy being around them. The Two wing tempers the Three's hunger to always be the winner. Genuine feelings come to the fore and powerful bonds of friendship can and will be formed.

A healthy Type Three with a Two wing can become an excellent motivational speaker, capable of inspiring great confidence and optimism in others. Uplifting and positive - think Tony Robbins or Oprah Winfrey at their best.

However, when unhealthy, a brittle vanity can come into play for the Achiever with a Two wing. They can lose touch with their genuine innermost feelings while instead constructing a false emotional facade. Self-promotion can become pushy and aggressive, resulting in a lose-lose situation for all involved. They might appear nice and quiet on the outside but the internal reality could be quite unpleasant and destructive.

As outer appearance is important, the 3W2 will typically dress well and in accordance with the latest mainstream fashion. This is because they will want to appeal to the largest possible audience. They might be drawn to "glamorous" work - perhaps on stage, TV, radio, or a high profile position in the business world.

Type Three with a Four Wing (3W4)

Although the Achiever with a Four wing would still like to be admired, they would prefer that this be for their uniqueness rather than appealing to the general masses - a select following rather than mass appeal is what they are aiming for.

The Four wing will tend to make the Three more introverted and less comfortable in social situations, although because of the still dominant Type Three personality, they will be able to hide this with their social competence. They will still be able to hold it all together in times of pressure.

A healthy and mature Achiever with a Four wing is compassionate, gentle and competent. This variant is wise and socially responsible and highly effective in accomplishing their goals, all the while remaining intuitive. A suitable job for this type would be as a career counsellor or a business mentor.

At their absolute best, the Type Three with a Four wing is quietly self-assured while possessed of stunning emotional insight. They teach through example, influencing others through compassionate action. They can be found at the top of organizations or behind the scenes, inspiring others to perform their best.

It is an entirely different story when the Achiever with a Four wing is immature and unhealthy. A lack of balance here will make the Three-influenced drive for success compulsive, while at the same time causing the introspection of the Four to get out of hand. Manipulation comes to the fore and the desire to help is no longer coming from a good place. They are not so great socially and may also indulge in self-deception. They might feel a compulsive need to tell other people about their accomplishments. At their worst, they can be destructive to the self and others.

They like to appear both attractive and unique, wanting to be trend-setters rather than slavishly following the latest fashion. The 3W4 variant is typically drawn to quite showy professions, such as music, politics, broadcasting, the stage, the fashion industry and the sales side of business.

Advice for the Achiever

Take a break every now and then from the relentless pursuit of your goals! Your health will benefit and so will your levels of happiness. And let's not forget your loved ones, who will all be pleased to have more time with you. Your goals will still be waiting for you when you wake up from a good night's sleep or return from a holiday. And you will feel refreshed and more effective than ever. Not to mention, nicer to be around. Ambition and determination can be sterling qualities, but they must be tempered by periods of rest which, additionally, allow time for you to reconnect deeply with your inner needs and feelings.

Try to be completely honest with yourself. Threes can sometimes get so caught up in trying to play to the peanut gallery that they lose touch with what they really need to be happy. Take time to consider what success actually means to you. What are your values? What makes you happy? Only when you truly connect with the reality of who you are, can you achieve real freedom.

As intimacy can sometimes be a challenge for you, it is worth taking the time and trouble to connect with a few chosen people on a deeper level. This takes self-awareness and the willingness to relax and practice appreciation for those you love.

It will benefit you greatly to become involved in projects that are unrelated to your ultimate ambition or career goals. It will take you outside of yourself in a healthy way and transcend your preoccupation with the opinions of others.

Chapter 6: Enneagram Type 1: The Perfectionist

The Perfectionist, sometimes known as the Reformer, constantly wants to see things improved—there is always something that can be done better, and nothing is ever quite good enough. They are idealistic in this sense—because they are always trying to improve everything around them, they are caught striving after an unachievable ideal. They want to make order in a world that is chaotic at heart, and this can be problematic.

If you have scored highly in the Type 1 Perfectionist, you likely have an eye for details and making sure that everything is just right. You are likely self-disciplined and will delay gratification if necessary, in order to ensure that the end result you are seeking comes to fruition. However, you also run into the problem of becoming too rigid and judgmental or even getting caught in your own self-righteousness with no hopes for escaping it.

Overview of the Perfectionist:

Before getting into a more in-depth analysis of the Perfectionist, let's take a moment to go over some basic information— below, you will find a list of the most basic information you can possibly get about the Type 1 individual. This is broken down into several categories to give you a brief snapshot into the mind of the Perfectionist.

Characteristic role: The Perfectionist

Ego fixation: Resentment

Holy idea: **Perfection**

Basic fear: Corruptness or imbalance

Basic desire: Integrity and balance

Temptation: Hypercritical or hypocritical

Vice: **Anger**

Virtue: **Serenity**

Direction of disintegration: Type 4: The Romantic

Direction of integration: Type 7: The Epicure

The Type 1 individual can be identified by several defining characteristics. These characteristics make the Type 1 individual the Perfectionist, including:

Often quite straightforward during interactions

Hyper-focused on practicality or being frugal

Hardworking and dedicated

Innately have high standards

Quite rigid when it comes to making plans

Can concentrate intensely

Natural talent for teaching

A Snapshot of the Perfectionist

In-person, the perfectionist is responsible—this is the person you see playing by the rules and ensuring that everything is exactly according to plan. They are quite serious and pragmatic. Despite how cold they may come across as when working diligently, they are quite dedicated to improving the welfare of others. They want to do better for the world, doing their best, and wielding their strengths in order to discover how best to achieve that improvement. They work behind the scenes, quietly and tenaciously controlling themselves, and they will go the extra mile to make sure that they always follow through with their promises to the best of their abilities.

The Perfectionist's Values

Above all, the Perfectionist values their own standards. They are intrinsically motivated—they want to do better because they want to improve everything around them. Their values and principles are important enough to push them forward without any extrinsic motivators, and they strive for responsibility and doing their due diligence. They seek to make sure that everyone is accountable and respect integrity. Their character is shaped largely by their sense of loyalty, justice, and honesty.

Recognizing the Perfectionist

When you are trying to spot the Perfectionist, you are looking for an organization. Because the Perfectionist strives for, well, perfection, their lives are usually quite orderly. They are usually clear-headed, honest, and deliberate—they feel obligated to provide those around them with the truth and seek to ensure that their ideals are achieved.

Thanks to their eye for justice and their passion for the rules and order, the Perfectionist is often found in fields that require a high sense of dedication and self-control. They are frequently found in the military, thriving on the sense of order and the hierarchy. They can be found in law with their passion for justice. They can be found in finance thanks to their meticulous attention to detail. They can be found in academia with their desire to improve society. No matter where you find them, however, one thing is true: The Perfectionist is always going to do everything in their power to perform as well as they can. They will make sure that they are meeting and exceeding standards at all costs and will methodologically follow the rules to a high standard, commonly making them some of the highest-performing individuals in their workplace.

The Perfectionist and Health

Of course, people's health fluctuates over time. It can go from healthy to average to unhealthy, and during each of these times, you will see different sides of the Perfectionist.

The Healthy Perfectionist

When healthy, the Perfectionist is able to use his or her strengths to their fullest potential. They are able to recognize that life around them is chaotic and constantly changing, and they are able to utilize their intense passion for changing and reforming the world around them to bring order to that chaos. They are able to use their strong sense of justice and what is fair to push humanity to its best potential. They are able to use their skills and self-control to figure out the perfect work-life balance, making sure that they take the time to relax when necessary between their pursuits to better the world around them.

The Average Perfectionist

When not quite at the best while far from the worst, the Perfectionist is able to organize life with ease. They are able to balance out aspects of their lives, compartmentalizing their needs, emotions, and drive to improve. Still just as passionate about bettering the world around them, the average Perfectionists are still pursuing life lived by their ideals and are usually quite involved in social events and causes that align with those ideals. They are usually quite professional, putting their entire beings into work, even going so far as suppressing their emotions and emotional needs for the greater good to get things finished.

The Unhealthy Perfectionist

When they become unhealthy, Perfectionists tend to start to lose touch with reality. They may become hyper-focused on matters that are rather irrelevant to their cause or argument. Of course, this can also very quickly spiral into an obsessive need to call out each and every little detail for discrepancies, seeking to discredit the opinions that do not line up with their own. They will do whatever they can to keep their own self-image upheld, making sure that they cannot possibly be wrong, even when they are. When they are challenged and feel like their values have been targeted, they may fly into a fit of rage in an attempt to defend them.

The Perfectionist's Strengths

The strengths and weaknesses of the Enneagram types can be broken down into five distinct categories: Physical, emotional, mental, relational, and spiritual.

Physical: They are able to identify moderation and live by it, balancing that need for perfection with the ability to relax and engage in self-care

Emotional: They can separate their desire for how things should be and accept things for how they are at that particular moment, recognizing that they cannot always control the end results

Mental: They are able to live true to their values, using their moral compasses to stay on target and driven toward doing the right thing, no matter how difficult it might be

Relational: They are able to inspire focus in other people, driving them and motivating them toward achieving their best as well

Spiritual: They are able to stay present without losing touch with their values

The Perfectionist's Weaknesses

Physical: Perfectionists typically engage in extremes—they under-eat or over or under-sleep. This puts them at risk for alcohol addiction

Emotional: They have a tendency to get caught up in the disappointment and displeasure toward their ideals not being achieved quickly enough, and maybe prone to OCD or depression

Mental: They get too caught up in black and white thinking, without recognizing the shades of grey that may play a part in what is happening around them

Relational: They are bothered by disorder and dislike making compromises, while also erring toward self-righteous and judgmental behavior as they get too critical

Spiritual: When they lose touch with their ideals, they tend to feel defective and corrupt, causing them to judge themselves harshly

The Perfectionist in a Relationship

In a relationship, the Perfectionist is quite detail-oriented. They love small gestures or when their partners are on time. When in a relationship with a Perfectionist, you must keep in mind to be respectful and ask for permission rather than assuming you have it. The Perfectionist wants to be noticed and complimented with something genuine, and they want someone that is just as dedicated to self-improvement.

When in this kind of relationship, it is important for you to acknowledge when you are wrong as soon as you realize that you are. Of course, this is only relevant when you are, in fact, wrong. By doing so, you are able to clear the air, and the Perfectionist's tendency for justice and integrity means that it will not be held against you.

It is important to remember that Perfectionists are largely workaholics—they are constantly dedicating themselves to bettering themselves and those around them, and they will work long hours. You must also attempt to avoid any sort of power struggles—it is possible for you both to be right, for yourselves, and those methods can coexist.

Chapter 7: Type Two - The Helper

Dominant Traits

- **Possessive**

- **Generous**

- **Demonstrative**

- **People-pleasers**

General Behavior

Ahelper is naturally a warm-hearted person. They are a fountain of empathy and are probably one of the most generous people you will meet. In a world that is so rough and unfriendly, an encounter with them can make you change your stance on life and feel that there is hope in the world after all.

Helpers value deep and true connections with people around them, which is why one of their key motivations is the desire to be loved. They perceive the world as a love-filled place where people appreciate each other for the deeds they do. The helper is also sometimes referred to as "the giver" in light of the one thing they love to do. Nothing can stop them from helping someone if they feel they can.

They feel most satisfied with their lives when they help as many people as they can. While this is generally a good thing, it can also be a negative drive. When helpers have a healthy affiliation, they are genuine in their support and will help out whenever they can. On the other hand, on the extreme end of the spectrum is a helper who derives the most satisfaction in appearing to help, even when they don't.

They generally feel that they need to prove their presence somewhere is necessary, so they go out of their way to assist. Their lives revolve around the things they feel deeply about, like meaningful friendships, their families, love, affection, and sharing whenever they can.

Helpers also tend to be overly involved in the lives of other people. All they want to do is help, but at times, this is not welcome, as some people might find their actions too intrusive. Compared to most of the other personality types, helpers have a healthy sense of balance in their lives. Their generosity and kindness know no bounds.

You will realize when interacting with a helper that they are people magnets. Their warmth and the fact that their actions are genuine makes people feel comfortable around them. People can share their problems with them without worrying about their issues blowing back in their faces.

One of the strongest identities of a helper is that as well as trying to do good, they also try to make people see the good within themselves. They will try to bring out the best in you so that you can believe in yourself and do well too. They believe that there is an element of positivity in everyone, even if you haven't realized it yet.

Typical Action Patterns

The life of a helper revolves around healthy, inclusive relationships. It fills them with so much joy to know that they are a part of something good, something that makes people happy. In a relationship with a helper, you will realize that they do their best to make things work. They will believe in the relationship more than anything else and would be broken if the relationship failed due to their failures.

However, it is not just about relationships, as helpers are also big on development. Both building something from scratch, and helping something blossom and achieve its true potential are amazing achievements in the life of a helper. They are very generous people, even when they barely realize they are doing it.

One of the good things about helpers is that they are genuine. As I'm sure you are aware, it is almost impossible to fake genuine generosity, because something soon irks you and your true intentions are revealed. However, this is not the case with helpers. Their concern is real, and when they help, they help because they believe it is the right thing to do. Hopefully, someday you might extend the same help to someone else in need.

While helpers will do all of this willingly and happily, this also makes life relatively difficult for them. There are many people who try to take advantage of their generosity, and they often end up unappreciated and used. They keep giving, and people keep taking.

Helpers will be there for anyone when they are in need of help. However, there are times when the helpers themselves need help but no one is in sight or chooses to help them. This still does not stop them from helping out where they can.

Some experts believe that helpers have a tendency to be very needy. This neediness comes from being worried that they are vulnerable, so instead of expressing their fears or their true emotions, they focus on what someone else needs. In this way, they take care of you and get their minds off the fact that they too are in need of help.

In situations where they deeply feel their needs are ignored, it is easier for them to dive deeper into the life of the person they are trying to help. The subconscious objective here is to remind you of their existence so that perhaps you can act accordingly and recognize their contributions.

Typical Thinking Patterns

One of the standout traits of a helper is that they try to assist people as much as they can. They are thoughtful, and will always try to put the needs of others ahead of theirs. This is the kind of person who will try their best to make you feel comfortable when you are going through a rough patch, without asking for anything in return.

As challenging as life is today, we all will encounter tragedy and crisis from time to time. In moments like this, many people are drawn to helpers because they seem to have a way of making things feel alright. They can help you come to terms with the reality of the changes going on in your life, easing the process of acceptance. Their words are thoughtful and considerate and will help you ease the pain.

The helper would probably fit within most religious parables, because of how they take care of the needs of others ahead of theirs. They are accommodating and can house you as you go through a turbulent moment in your life. If you need someone to talk to, this is the person you reach out to. They will listen, comfort you, and remind you that you are valuable, you are important, and you deserve the good things in life.

Since they love to take care of people and things around them, their nurturing element is also drawn to plants, animals, and children. Children, especially infants, have an instinctive attraction to people who emit positive vibes. This explains why they suddenly calm down when they are around helpers.

As you interact with such an individual, you will realize that they are very careful in the way they speak. They will be so attuned to your pain that they try to say the right things even when the situation makes it very difficult for them to do so. In a group setting, they will be seen as the indispensable members, because they offer comfort as no one else can. The groups need them in difficult times to offer reassurance that everything will be okay.

Typical Feeling Patterns

Helpers feel deeply towards others. If they are in a relationship, they embrace all the emotions that come with being in that partnership. This is something that can make them vulnerable, but there is not much they can do about this. One of their biggest challenges is that while they feel happiness, hurt, and every other emotion and sentiment, they tend to block themselves from recognizing their own needs.

It is important that in this situation, the helper realizes that they are just as human as everyone else, and they also need to be taken care of. When there is no reciprocity in a relationship, it easily becomes a negative and one-sided experience.

For helpers, they often shy away from living their own experiences. Instead, they insert themselves into other people's problems. Instead of dealing with their shortcomings, they find someone else whose shortcomings are more apparent and help them fix their situation. These are people who have too much love to give, but end up with very little love for themselves.

Feelings and emotions are a normal part of life. Growth in your life as a helper will only come when you embrace these feelings for yourself in the same way that you do for everyone else. There is much you will be able to achieve in life once you rise above this and start treating yourself as well as you treat everyone else.

In most societies, helpers are caregivers. You will find them as social support workers or working in nursing facilities. They love to teach, whether in formal or informal settings.

As a helper, you should learn to recognize your own weaknesses and strengths. Realize that you are vulnerable and need help, and ask for help when it is necessary. Only then will you truly be able to help people as you love to because you won't only see them as people who need help and who you can help, but you will also understand what they are going through.

Helpers appreciate very deep and meaningful relationships, connections and friendships. Their generosity knows no bounds, and they are always ready to support anyone without undermining their position or their feelings.

How to Improve Your Life

Your willingness to help people is commendable. However, other people will not always appreciate it as they may feel you are too imposing or focusing too much on their lives, and become irritated. From time to time, you tune yourself into other people's feelings, allowing you to understand them and offer your support. Rejection will affect you badly, so ask for consent before you offer to help. Don't just volunteer to help, ask the person whether they need your help and, if so, how they would like you to assist.

Why are you so interested in helping people? Question your motives to make sure you are genuine in your intentions. Helping someone from the purity of your heart is a good thing. However, if you are only helping them so that they can be indebted to you or so that you receive praise and admiration from them, you are not doing it for the right reasons. You don't want to end up in a cycle where your life revolves around seeking approval from the people you help.

Try to picture of yourself outside the helping dynamic. Are you trying to meet your personal needs to the same extent that you are helping someone else and meet their needs? As much as your help is appreciated, it is not always recommended. Remind yourself that you cannot satisfy everyone's needs. Therefore, do only what you can, then be on your way and don't feel guilty.

People show affection and appreciation in different ways. In your interactions, learn to identify this feedback so that you recognize how receptive they are to you.

People who care about you can show it in more ways than you know. This knowledge is a reminder that they value you.

Chapter 8: Coping Strategies For Empaths

Coping as an empath is probably one of the single most important things that you will ever learn about. With the right coping methods, you can ensure that you are not being overwhelmed by your gifts and having them run amuck on you. This way, you can always feel confident in your ability to stay in control over yourself and your energies even in the most challenging of environments. In this chapter, you are going to explore what your unique coping needs are, how to create your coping goals and strategies that you can use to begin coping better.

Your Unique Coping Needs

The first thing that you need to know is what your unique coping needs are as an empath. While the general purpose of coping will always remain the same, each empath may find that their unique needs are different based on how they experience their empathic gifts. In order to discover what you need in order to help you cope, you should start by considering the areas in life that you struggle with the most. This way, you can start to identify where coping methods may be needed based on what specifically is making your empathic gift so challenging to manage.

A great way to discover where your struggles are to refer back to your journal and start considering what is causing the most problems for you. Then, see if you can identify why and what part of your empathic gifts are being overwhelmed during those particular moments. You may find that you struggle most with dealing with other people's emotions or energies, or that you find yourself being dragged down by the collective energy of an environment in general. You may find that there are even specific people or types of people who are hard for you to be around but due to circumstances beyond your control, you may have to be around these people on a consistent basis. By identifying exactly where your empathic gifts become the most challenging, you can discover exactly what you need to do in order to overcome those challenges and experience greater success in managing your empathic gifts.

The Goal of Coping Strategies

Once you have identified where you struggle the most in your life, you need to start identifying what specific goals you want to be working towards so that you know what you are trying to achieve through your coping strategies. Your goals should directly align with your challenges outlined in the previous section to ensure that you are working on things that actually matter to your unique needs. If you have many areas of your life where you need to improve your coping strategies, consider starting with the parts of your life that pose the biggest challenges for you. That way, the relief that you are working towards has a massive impact on your life from the start, and you can move on to managing the less challenging but still difficult parts of your life after.

Coping Strategies for You to Try

There are many coping methods that you can try when it comes to coping with your empathic struggles. Some we have already covered in previous chapters, whereas, others will be discovered below. The more coping strategies you equip yourself with, the easier it will be for you to overcome challenges and move forward. Take your time and practice each of these coping methods, starting with the ones that serve your needs first and then moving on to learning how to incorporate the rest of these coping methods later.

Quiet Time Outside

As an empath, being in nature is a great way to cope with your daily challenges as nature tends to have a very healing and relaxing energy that is not present in crowded areas within society. As a general rule of thumb, retreating to be in nature at least once or twice a week is a great opportunity for you to completely ground your energies and restore your inner sense of peace. While you are there, you can either walk or simply allow yourself to be present in nature, or you can set aside some time to meditate and allow yourself to intentionally ground and bring in peace through your meditation. If you are someone who prefers comfort and familiarity, consider finding an area near your home that you can go on a regular basis, such as a forest or a riverside. Going to the same space each time can amplify its healing effect by helping you stay more focused and intentional while you are there. It can also help by having you know exactly what energy to expect while you are in the area so that the energy associated with "new" or different surroundings do not interrupt your grounding abilities.

Alone Time

As you know, solitude is one of the greatest tools that you can use when it comes to managing your energies and thriving as an empath. This coping method can be used by spending more time alone doing calm activities by yourself, or it can be used on-the-go if you are in need of a quick refresh from a challenging day. A great opportunity to tap into alone time on the go is by going outside for a few minutes, going to the bathroom for a few minutes, or even retreating to your office and closing the door for a few minutes when you need to. Giving yourself these few minutes of alone time will greatly help you relax and recharge after a particularly challenging time. Plus, you only need a couple of minutes to generate a sense of inner peace and restore yourself so that you can go about your day as usual and not feel so overwhelmed.

When you first start using short bursts of alone time to help you get through your day, you may feel like a few minutes is not enough and you are still overwhelmed when you go back to your daily routine. Trust that this is normal: you have not yet taught your mind and body to recognize that these breaks are a part of your new normal and that you will have another one soon. The more you use these breaks, the more your mind will be able to relax because it will trust that another break can be had soon if you feel that you need it again. This sense of inner trust cultivates a deeper sense of inner peace and will help you cope better overall.

Emotional Expression

As an empath, you pick up a lot of emotions from your day-to-day experiences, which is probably one of the most challenging parts of being an empath. Despite the fact that these emotions are not always yours, they are experienced as if they were which means that you need to practice proper emotional expression to help yourself release the emotions you carry. Some empaths like to express their emotions immediately, whereas, others like to use intentional expression time as an opportunity to express their emotions. However you choose to do it, make sure that you set aside time for you to completely feel and release your emotions.

The more you intentionally release your emotions, the less you will carry within you. This continuous expression prevents emotions and energies from building up within you so that your inner bottle does not remain "full," thus making further emotional experiences even harder to navigate. Instead, your inner emotional reservoir remains balanced so that you can experience new emotions without having them piggyback on others and increase your challenges in navigating your emotions.

Maintain a Healthy Lifestyle

One way to balance your empathic gifts is to maintain a healthier lifestyle and focus on your overall well-being. When we do not manage our general health, stress hormones like cortisol and adrenaline increase which can result in you feeling an intense amount of general overwhelm within. As a result, managing your emotions also becomes more challenging because you are experiencing so much overall stress.

As an empath, one of the biggest things you can do aside from eating a healthy diet, getting a good sleep, and exercising on a regular basis is to drink plenty of water. From a spiritual aspect, water is the element that resembles emotions and drinking water will help you move unwanted energy through your body and release challenging emotions from your system. Staying hydrated will not only help your general health, but it will also help with the passing energy and emotion through your system so that you can heal from your inner emotional challenges as an empath.

Try Yoga

Yoga is a profound and powerful way of navigating your energies and emotions as an empath. Yoga itself involves gentle exercise with meditation and intentional breathing to help move energy through your body and keep you in a calm and centered state of being. If you want to get everything you can gain from yoga, choose a particular style of yoga such as Hatha or Bikram yoga and commit yourself not only to engaging in the exercises but also in the learning of it. Each style of yoga features theory and education around energy, including the management and processing of energy, which means that a good yoga practice will help you stay in shape while also managing your empathic energies. This makes this an especially powerful form of activity for empaths to engage in.

If you are not overly confident in practicing yoga with a group of people, you may wish to incorporate yoga into your solitude practices. Spending time alone deeply engaged in a yoga practice can give you the restorative benefits of being alone alongside the benefits of yoga itself, which ultimately supercharges these two coping methods.

Use Guided Meditations

Guided meditations are another great way for you to manage specific types of energy. If you find yourself being bogged down by a specific energy, such as the energy of anger or envy, consider using guided meditations as an opportunity to help yourself release these energies and move on from them. YouTube is filled with plenty of great guided meditations that you can follow that range from fifteen minutes to sixty minutes in length. To engage in one, simply relax into a comfortable sitting or lying down position and turn one on then follow the instructions of the person guiding the meditation. It may take a few tries to find someone who has a voice that you can actually relax to, but once you do, you may find that this is one of your best coping methods yet.

The best part about guided meditations is that they tend to be extremely versatile and they can help you move through just about anything that you may be facing. If you feel that you do not currently have an effective coping method towards a specific type of energy, engaging in a guided meditation is a great opportunity for you to expand your skillset. As you do, you may find yourself naturally engaging in inner meditations any time you experience a specific type of unwanted energy, based on what you learned in a guided video. These guided meditations often feature visualizations that coincide with the releasing of unwanted energies, which is what makes them so powerful in the long run. The more you engage in them, the more visualization you will discover and the more likely you will be to discover a certain visualization that really helps you cope with certain energies. This way, you can simply recall that visualization practice and use it at any given time to help you through an energetic release, even if you are on the go.

Your Quick Start Action Step: Your Signature Coping Method

Now that you have a general sense of what you can do to cope with unwanted energies, it is time for you to develop your "signature coping method!" As an empath, one of the greatest things that you can do for your energy is to use a consistent routine when it comes to releasing unwanted energies. The reason for this is that, not only is it a good way to rely on things that actually work, but it also increases their functionality because your brain becomes used to associating particular coping strategies with an energetic release. As a result, your strategies will actually work quicker and will have a deeper impact on helping you release overall.

To develop your signature coping method, consider your goals once again and pick a strategy listed above that works best in helping you achieve that specific goal. Then, go ahead and begin practicing that method on a regular basis. As you do, you may find that you want to customize it to fit your needs a little better, which will help you make it your signature strategy. The more you practice it and personalize it for your own needs, the greater fulfillment you will gain from it, so make sure that you practice it on a regular basis.

Notice how much more powerful it becomes as you do, and lean into that power to further enhance your ability to cope using your signature coping strategy.

Chapter 9: Your Enneagram Type:

Personality Test

Finding out your core personality type in truth is not a short process and it is something which takes time and thought. There are countless Enneagram tests online which will help you gain some insight, and the RHETI (Riso-Hudson Enneagram Type Indicator) is the most commonly used. This particular test has been scientifically validated, and is thought to be around 80% accurate in most cases. On top of this, another credible source is the TAS Questionnaire in The Wisdom of Enneagram. Again, this is scientifically validated, and offers the same high level of accuracy.

There are many shorter online personality tests you can take, if you want to simply start thinking about what type of personality you are, before giving in to self-reflection to truly arrive at the most accurate result for you.

To break it down into more simplistic terms:

• Think carefully, think about how you react, how you feel, and how you behave on a daily basis

• Be totally and brutally honest, even ask a close friend or family member to list your attributes and behavior patterns if that helps

• Take an online personality test and assess the results – do you agree with them?

• Use a scientifically validated test, such as the TAS Questionnaire, or the RHETI, which we mentioned above

• Think a little more – do you agree with the results? It's important to realize that you might be surprised, so don't discount the results because you simply don't think you display a certain characteristic; you might have it without realizing! Again, ask a close friend or family member for advice

Once you have gone through this process you should finally come up with a type which reflects you.

We are rarely purely one type. Throughout your decision journey, it's important to note that we are very rarely one type only; we are complicated beings, and therefore we display characteristics of various types – however with that in mind, there should be one type which comes up time and time again, and that is your core personality type.

Whilst we are all born with one particular main type within us, it's likely that this doesn't really show itself too much until the teenage years appear which we all know is a time of experiment and self-discovery in itself. During the 20s, the main personality type will show itself more so, and this is when the Enneagram becomes much easier to pinpoint.

Once you realize which personality type you truly are, the journey certainly does not end there.

The whole point of the Enneagram is to use your personality type results to help you understand your inner being in a much more detailed way. Once you figure out which is your main personality type, this is just step one on your journey to self-discovery, self-development, and self-enlightenment.

You can use your results to pinpoint the negative parts of your personality and improve upon them. However, it's also worthwhile knowing that everyone has their faults so the Enneagram is never going to make you a 100% perfect person. On top of this, understanding your strengths by pinpointing your personality type can allow you to develop them further, and use them for good, rather than negative causes.

Take the test now and once you've gotten your results, go back to section II to read a more in-depth description of your type then jump into section III to figure out what kind of a layered cake you have.

To access the test, simply copy and paste the following link into your browser:

What are Levels of Development?

If you have read anything about the Enneagram before, you might have heard of Levels of Development, and you might be wondering what this is all about.

Once you pinpoint your core personality type, you can begin your journey into developing your understanding, using the results to develop as a person. Levels of Development therefore describe how an individual's personality type shifts and changes as they become more familiar with it, and as they develop more as a person overall.

Over time, everyone heads upwards and downwards within the line level of their particular personality type, and this changes especially as an individual becomes more **au fait** with their type, and as a result, their true inner being.

Are you ready to learn more about the different personality types?

Of course, you could also argue that understanding all nine personality types can help you in your social life too, as understanding other people is key to having healthy, functioning relationships, in your personal, work, and social lives.

Remember we said the subtypes are like layers of a cake that we all have?

That implies you already possess all three basic instincts, but one will be more dominant. By discovering how your cake is layered, you'll start to be more awake in your daily life choices, and some of your impulses, reactions, and experiences will make more sense.

Your personality type combined with your wings and center as well as your basic instincts layered up now give you a detailed understanding of what makes you tick. And what a liberation that becomes as you step into improving your relationships with others.

Chapter 10: The Individualist

The primary words used to describe an individualist are dramatic, expressive, temperamental, and self-absorbed. The growth line for a type four personality moves to a type one personality. The stress line moves from a type four to a type two personality. Some famous people with type four personalities include Johnny Depp, Kate Winslet, Amy Winehouse, Billie Holiday, Judy Garland, Anne Frank, and Hank Williams ("Type Four," n.d.).

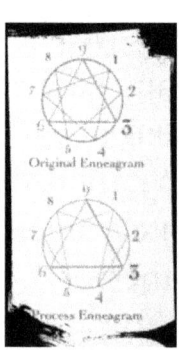

What is the Individualist?

Type four personalities are known to be extremely sensitive to what is going on around them. They tend to feel emotions deeply. In fact, most feel emotions on a deeper level than other personalities. Of course, this can cause problems when it comes to a type four because they can have trouble controlling their feelings, which can become overwhelming. Because of this, the individualist will need to use certain techniques, so they can manage the stress of their emotions.

Because of how overwhelming emotions can be, the individualist will withdraw from society. They will usually have a select group of friends they regularly see and talk to, and they tend to withdraw from others. Their overwhelming emotions can also cause them to feel self—pity, melancholy, or become severely depressed. Just because type four personalities tend to withdraw from society, doesn't mean they want to be alone in their life. Unfortunately, because of their lack of social life, they often begin to feel this way which can increase their depression or internal sadness. At the same time, because individualists are concerned about their self-image, they will often become anxious when in a social setting. They are afraid of making a mistake that will cause people to judge them or think that they are socially awkward, which will deter them from social settings ("Type Four," n.d.).

The biggest struggle a type four has in regard to their emotions is letting go of the past. They often feel guilty over mistakes they have made, especially if it negatively affected their self-image. On top of this, they genuinely struggle with letting go of emotions. Therefore, type four personalities can hold on to emotions for years, if not longer.

Their main desire is to feel that they have significance ("Type Four," n.d.). They want to be sure they have an identity in the world and be able to understand themselves. When it comes to their biggest fear, which is also their strongest emotion, they worry about their identity and what special features they have. They want to do something special and become noticed. Therefore, they are often worried about their personal significance and fear that they have none.

The reason why this fear is so extreme for the individualist is because they know they aren't like other people. They believe they are different, which makes them believe that others cannot understand them. While they know they possess unique and one-of-a-kind talents, they also believe that they are uniquely flawed. Because of this, they tend to become more aware of their unique characteristics more than other people. They also make sure to take care of these characteristics more than most people. Individualists believe that their unique characteristics are some of the most important features of their personality ("Type Four," n.d.).

Type four personalities are often motivated when they are able to express their individuality. They also like to see the beauty in the world and will often surround themselves with what they find beautiful. They also receive motivation when they are allowed to take care of themselves before they need to take care of someone else. However, they enjoy knowing that they are about to help other people ("Type Four," n.d.).

Other than becoming overwhelmed with emotions, individualists often think that they are missing something in their life. Unfortunately, they never fully grasp an idea of what they are missing. Therefore, they think it can be a variety of factors and will often try different careers or change aspects of their personality to figure out what is missing ("Type Four," n.d.). For example, some might think they don't have enough friends, so they will start to become more social. Other individualists might think that they are missing a piece of themselves, such as self-confidence, so they will start to increase their confidence.

A couple of the biggest problems individualists face with themselves is their lack of self-esteem and poor self-image. Both of these factors tend to negatively affect individualists in several ways throughout their life. For example, it can be what causes them to become socially withdrawn, not use their talent to its fullest potential, or become afraid to try something new out of fear of what it will do to their self-image. Because of this, they will often compensate by creating an idealized image of themselves. They use this image as someone they want others to see them as. They will also use this imaginary version of themselves to become the best person they can be.

Levels of Integration

Healthy Level

The highest level for an individualist is level one, which means that they are able to let go of their past emotions, realize they have a positive self-image, and are able to take all their life experiences and transform them into something special and valuable. These experiences are able to help them learn and grow, which is what they focus on when they are transforming. They also realize they are very unique and creative people, and are not shy about expressing themselves, whether it is through art, music, or writing (Cloete, n.d.).

At a level two, individualists are known to be extremely gentle, sensitive, and compassionate. They are aware that they internalize feelings deeply and use techniques in order to help themselves manage the feeling of becoming overwhelmed with emotion. They are comfortable with their self-image, but also believe that they still need to improve themselves. Furthermore, they still continue to search for who they really are (Cloete, n.d.).

An individualist who is at a level three, is honest with themselves and others. They are self-aware of their emotions but often overcome their overwhelming feeling with humor. In fact, they are known to not be very serious people because they tend to find humor in almost anything. Even if they think their self-image has drawn on some negativity, they realize that this happens because no one is perfect and people make mistakes. Therefore, they are known to remain true to themselves (Cloete, n.d.).

Average Level

A type four who is at a level four tends to use their creative abilities to overcome their strong feelings. They are also known to be the most romantic individualists. Like others, they focus on creating a beautiful environment around them, even if they have to create a fantasy to do this. They are known to have an active imagination but do their best to remain true to their passionate emotions (Cloete, n.d.).

Individualists who are at a level five tend to take everything personally and have trouble separating what isn't aimed at them and what is. Because of this, they are perceived to be very self-absorbed people but, in reality, they are hypersensitive. They are also very self-conscious and shy, which makes it hard for them to become spontaneous. They are considered to be introverted. They often don't spend a lot of time in social settings because it helps them protect their self-image. Another reason they are introverted is because it allows them to control their emotions better because they are able to out their emotions (Cloete, n.d.).

A type four who is at a level six tends to focus more on self-pity because they realize they are different, which means they cannot live the same way as other people do. Because of this, they will often create a happier and healthier fantasy world. Other people tend to view a level six as self-indulgent and unproductive. At the same time, they are also viewed as dreamers and unique individuals (Cloete, n.d.).

Unhealthy Level

One of the unhealthy levels for a type four is a level seven. At this level, individualists tend to get very angry with themselves, which makes them become socially withdrawn. Because of this, they often struggle with depression. Furthermore, they start to feel ashamed by their overwhelming emotions, which makes them block out their emotions. A level seven will often struggle with daily functioning because they often feel exhausted. Individualists will start to reach this level when their fantasy world fails and they can no longer imagine a happier world for themselves (Cloete, n.d.).

A level eight often starts to feel tormented by their self-image. These individualists usually have very low self-esteem and often blame others for their problems. At this level, individualists tend to hate themselves and think melancholy. They will often push away anyone who tries to help them for several reasons, such as wanting to be alone or feeling like they don't deserve the help (Cloete, n.d.).

The highest level that individualists can reach is a level nine. Type four personalities who reach this level typically have problems with drugs and alcohol as this helps them cope with their morbid thoughts and low self-esteem. They often find themselves contemplating suicide and suffer from various mental diseases such as narcissistic and avoidant personality disorders (Cloete, n.d.).

Subtypes of the Individualist

Social Category is Shame

Shame is the basic emotion for a type four personality. Therefore, this emotion shows up in their daily lives constantly. In fact, they can quickly make themselves feel guilty, which will cause them to also feel ashamed. While they are not competitive, they do like people telling them they are positively influencing other people in society. They like to know their self-worth as this helps them understand who they are. Socially, they are open to people when it comes to the shame they feel, which makes people admire and support individualists. This will often boost the confidence of a type four because they are quick to doubt themselves and their abilities (Cloete, n.d.).

Self-Preservation Category is Tenacity

Tenacity is the countertype for individualists and often makes people mistake them for a type one or type seven personality. Through self-preservation, type four personalities learn to live with their suffering, with some finding ways to overcome it. In fact, they often believe that it is their suffering which has made them stronger and able to manage various life circumstances. Because of this, they will often look for other people who they believe suffer in the same way they have so they can become a support system for them (Cloete, n.d.).

One-on-One Category is Competition

Type four personalities are not competitive when it comes to sports. Their competitive nature comes out when they have demands and want attention from other people in order to prove their self-worth. They become competitive when it comes to other people believing they are helpful, sensitive, compassionate, and generous individuals. Furthermore, individualists can become demanding when it comes to wanting people to listen to their emotions. In a sense, individualists want people to understand what they need and appreciate the struggles they face as sensitive people (Cloete, n.d.).

Relationships with Other Types

Depending on what level of integration individualists are in will influence how well they get along with other types. If they are at the healthiest level of integration, they can get along with nearly all the other personalities. However, when they are at a lower average and unhealthy level they will be less likely to have a healthy relationship with other personalities ("Relationships (Type Combinations)," n.d.).

Wing Types

One of the wings for type four personalities is type three. The advantages that the achievers bring to the individualists are helping them express their creative fantasies. Because of the type three personality, type four is able to balance their internal drama so that they can become more social. When they do reach their social setting, achievers will help them express their unique selves in a way that can engage other people. On top of this, type three will help the type four transform their life experiences in a positive way. The challenges that achievements bring to individualists are the feelings of having to hide their emotions and internalizing them as a way to control them. Achievers can also increase the feeling of sadness that type four personalities have because of the pressure individualists will feel towards achieving a certain level of success (Cloete, n.d.).

The second wing for individualists is type five. When it comes to the advantages that type five brings, it is teaching individualists to take things less personally. They also help them control their emotions and help them feel less detached from the world. On top of this, they can help them think logically and observe society objectively. The challenges that individualists face with type five are overdramatizing their self-image in a negative way, struggling to connect with other people, and becoming more withdrawn from society so they can hide their emotions easier (Cloete, n.d.).

Center Points

Individualists are part of the heart center. If you have a type four personality, you want to know why you are different from other people (Cloete, n.d.). You are proud of your individuality, which can be both a strength and weakness towards your character. Furthermore, type fours tend to internalize their shame, which is often how they begin to create their unique character.

Type four's strengths:

- Compassion
- Feeling deeply
- Empathy
- Creative
- Idealistic

Type four's weaknesses:

- Overly sensitive
- Dissatisfaction
- Demanding
- Self-absorbed
- Withdrawn
- Moody

How to Grow Personally

Keep Your Thoughts Positive

Keeping your thoughts positive will help you stay in the right mindset and avoid lengthy negative conversations with your imagination. Once you are able to accomplish this, you will begin to increase your self-esteem and confidence. Over time, you will find that you are able to turn negative life experiences into more positive experiences, which will help you grow and learn as an individualist.

One of the facts about being a type four personality, is you might never feel like you've found your true place in this world. You will often feel, whether you admit it to yourself or not, that you are unique and hold special characteristics unlike many other people. When you start to feel this way, you have to remember to maintain a positive mindset. You need to realize that the best thing you can do is remain unique but not allow yourself to become too withdrawn from society (Cloete, n.d.).

Use Self-Discipline to Help Manage Your Emotions

When you use self-discipline in your daily life, you will find that you start to feel less stressed and are able to manage your emotions better. It is important to know that self-discipline can show itself in many forms, from following a daily schedule to make sure you take time to meditate or any other way to release your negative emotions. For example, you will want to get enough sleep so that you will be better able to manage your emotions and struggles of being highly sensitive and individualistic. Furthermore, making sure that you find time for yourself so you can release any negativity will help you gain better control over transforming your negative thoughts into positive ones (Cloete, n.d.).

Don't Procrastinate

Another helpful way to grow your personality is to not procrastinate. Part of this you will learn through self-discipline.

The other part you will learn as you stop procrastinating. Individualists will often put off tasks until they feel ready to do them. This happens because they feel like they have to prepare themselves in order to take on what they need to accomplish. However, there is never truly a correct time to do everything, especially if you are not looking forward to what you are doing.

Procrastination can make your emotions stronger, especially when it comes to negative emotions, such as stress. Therefore, once you stop procrastinating and start working on your tasks when you need to, you will find you are more capable of handling your emotions. Furthermore, you will start to gain self-confidence and believe that your self-image is more positive overall. Procrastination can interfere with a positive mindset, therefore, you want to do what you can to work on your tasks as soon as possible (Cloete, n.d.).

Chapter 11: Know Your Instincts To Be

Appreciated By Others

Now the time has come to discover a great truth that does not always come out of people's lives.

Self-conscious people give importance to the right things and do not get lost in insignificant moments of their lives.

All those who work seriously and constantly on themselves have a knowledge of the mechanisms of their own personality that allows them to have greater confidence in themselves, a confidence that comes from within and not from outside - or if we prefer - which comes from a place that is true and not illusory.

Therefore they do not lose themselves in futile things, they do not try to make you feel inferior or attack you where you are weakest. They do not feel threatened or jealous. They know their limits and do not hide them.

Self-awareness is the basis of all those qualities that we aspire to see in the people we love most, the partner, children, parents and our friends. You know who you are and trust that the other person knows himself. Being kind becomes easier because we understand and make the other's emotions our own. This is empathy. Since you spend time processing your emotions you will also be more emotionally available and instead of feeling threatened, misunderstood and closed, you will be able to dedicate yourself to more authentic and sincere relationships.

The key to understanding the other person (children, parents, brothers, etc.) and connecting with it with renewed clarity lies within ourselves. After all, who wouldn't want a sincere partner? Well this will be your next "golden rule" for when you look for one - make sure you're the sincere partner.

Self-conscious people are nicer. In fact it is quite obvious if you think about your direct experiences or your knowledge that a self-aware companion or companion can become a real blast because they understand what makes living fun. They can be self-ironic and capable of making fun of themselves, not because they are insecure but because they understand their own gaps and limitations and are willing to put them out in the open instead of creating a false image of self-confident people.

A self-conscious person is a person who knows the right value of sincerity and will not lie to you. He will not tell you a comfortable lie in order not to "hurt your feelings." In an intimate relationship we need our counterpart to tell us things frankly. If we can't trust in intimate relationships what can we trust in the end? Conscious people are clear about their intentions and what they want. After seeing the painful effects that lies and dishonesty create in a relationship, you immediately recognize that the wisest thing to do is to refuse to create further garbage. Self-awareness can come out as something grumpy or too abrupt, but it's true - and what's real is always the best thing.

In today's world we live in a wrong dimension of empathy and only those who internalize the emotions of others can understand the pain and suffering that exists in the world. A self-conscious person is aware of what is around her at such a point that empathy goes to a higher level. People thus create better friendships and bonds because they respect and wonder at the human experience of each one. All this creates a sense of meaning and connection that most people do not have.

Now let's talk about self-preservation. It is a word that includes a wonderful ancestral concept: man has an intimate power, a force within himself that leads him on a path of protection against dangers. It is a tendency that oscillates between the very strong desire not to change a situation in which man's life is protected and a dimension of eternal search for new perspectives to get better and go into a better situation for himself and his family.

All people have something to protect and they want to protect themselves from external forces. In the moment in which certain actions are put in place to feel in a refuge far from the dangers of the world and of life, then it is the moment in which the instinct of self-preservation presents itself in all its wonderful ancestral ability.

The person who preserves himself adequately proves to be grateful for the enormous gift of life and is also responsible for treating him well and in a respectful way, as animals do, even those with simpler cell structures.

Preserving one's life and respecting other life forms is, after all, one of the most basic attitudes expected of all living beings. Among animals, in Nature, one kills only for one's own survival and preserves life in the most diverse ways, avoiding predators.

Furthermore, considering the level closest to the true entity of a human being and its healthier functioning, the self-conservative instinct is linked to the contemplative capacity and the most profound contact with silence. Another interesting element is the realization that it is very important to engage the body in the processes of development of consciousness.

Being "present" is the basis of the practice of those who invest in spiritual development, starting with the ability to feel totally connected to the body.

However, those who are exaggerated - the dominant self-preservatives - carry with them, if possible, a shadow of lack of confidence in life, thus defining a sort of attitude of greater distrust before destiny.

On the other hand, those who are insufficiently preserved - repressed self-preservatives - can have a similar shadow of mistrust on the fact that there is no one who provides what is necessary and does not help to adequately preserve life.

Both profiles often bring with them central traumas of episodes in which life has been threatened. Some examples of common traumas seen during the most profound workshops with the Enneagram are: physical, health or survival risks perceived during childhood or in the intrauterine period; ancient situations of lack of resources or deprivation; memories of systemic or even collective family pains related to hunger, death by war and scarcity.

The self-conservative instinct is obviously connected to the world of the mother who protects her children, the lioness who keeps her puppies safe, the mother who hugs and nurses children. The mother has the archetypal function of protecting the

137

offspring and at the tribal level she preserves and protects life, the heirs of the social group and therefore the possibility of a specific whole social group to move forward into the future and establish a connection between present and future. Working on the relationship with the mother to resolve any trauma of this relationship is, for various reasons, indispensable for all those who place themselves on the path of self-development.

Sometimes it happens that the issues related to the mother tend to be perceived by the individual as more traumatic when the self-conservative instinct is dominant. Often there are cases in which individuals feel an addiction and an excessive attachment to the maternal figure compared to when the self-conservative instinct is repressed, where a probable excessive detachment from the maternal figure is generated.

The almost permanent, conscious or unconscious feeling of people who are dominant self-conservative is one in which life is threatened and something risky for survival can happen at any time. In practice, this feeling leads this group of people to have a more anxious, wary, risk-averse and pragmatic trait compared to other people of the same type as the Enneagram.

Quality of organization, punctuality and regularity are also common in dominant self-preservatives. People like this also tend to worry at least a little more with their health and with financial issues and controls. These people also tend to pay more attention to themselves and their priorities, compared to colleagues of the same type. As a side effect, I am at greater risk of being individualistic and having a shadow of egoism or even opportunism. The style tends to be more self-sufficient and introverted - however, always taking as a reference, in this comparison, the other colleagues of the same type.

Those who are repressed self-preservatives may have a tendency not to consider their lives as sufficiently important and, therefore, the subject of well-deserved care. With this, these people can demonstrate, in a voluntary or involuntary (active or passive) way, a certain negligence and even a contempt for life - mainly towards everyday life. On the other hand, there is a profile of audacity, risk appetite and a possible courageous entrepreneur attitude (while a dominant self-conservative can have more the profile of the manager rather than the entrepreneur).

Distraction, disorganization and aversion to routine can easily become weaknesses for these people, as well as a certain lack of attention to health issues and an obedience to the needs of the body. When compared to colleagues of the same type as the Enneagram, these people tend to be more extroverted.

Here is an exercise for you. I want you to think about your instincts to help you be more aware of yourself and all that surrounds you without the prejudices of the superstructures in which we live.

Premise for the success of the exercise: always look for honesty with yourself. Don't lie, it's useless. Lies are useless and take you away from your goal of a peaceful future.

Exercise: Take a notebook, choose a nice notebook that you like because it will become a small companion of adventures every day. Every day you write the date and write the things you did accompanying them by the instinct that guided your actions according to you. Put an asterisk next to the actions you could have done better and that you could have lived with a better mood.

Chapter 12: The Enneagram Test

This test is approximately thirty questions long, and primarily seeks to identify your base personality of the nine under the enneagram model. For every question, record your answer separately, whether on a piece of paper or digitally, any way where you can go back and read through the answer later. Ideally, answers to the questions on this test are "yes", "no", or "neutral/I don't know". Your results will be based on which of the sentiments you most relate to, and which questions you feel more of a direct connection to. Do not think about the questions for longer than you absolutely need to—personality tests give the clearest and most accurate results when the answers are immediate, I.e. the most honest they can be. So, let's start.

Do you feel as though people around you might be suspicious of you, or are holding some kind of important information from you?

If someone comes up to you and begins to provoke you, specifically on a topic that you feel very sensitively about, would your immediate impulse be to fight back, or to instigate a further argument or physical fight with the other person?

Do you friends, family, loved ones, etc. find you to be rigid, or describe you as cold or distant, or overly harsh?

Do you believe your achievements are more important to have to yourself than they are to show off to others?

Do you get a rush of excitement or feel very accomplished with yourself when you feel like you've made someone you look up to proud of you, like a parent or a teacher?

Do you find yourself prone to being lost in thought often, daydreaming off in another world, even if something relatively important may be happening in front of you?

Does it feel like your main purpose in groups is to calm others down and make sure no one gets into a fight?

Are you underappreciated?

Are you the life of the party?

Would you be willing to put yourself in harm's way for the comfort of a friend or family member, even if the potential risk is greater to you than the benefit to them?

Do you think your human experience is separate from those of others, or that your life is hard to understand to outside people?

Do you find yourself feeling like you have to be the one who makes the decisions for other people, and do you enjoy that role?

Do you think you enjoy having achievements because of the status, as opposed to the work you had to do to get the approval that came with the achievement?

Do you feel bad about yourself, or like you've failed others, when you can't stand up for what you believe in or defend others in a public setting?

Are you the kind of person who likes arguing, or who would go out of their way to find someone who you know disagrees with you, so that you can engage them in some kind of disagreement?

Do you act the way you do, or follow rules, out of principle before you actually consider those rules in the context of your own moral compass of the moral compass of other people?

Do you feel as though you're always thinking about multiple things at once, or like you think too fast for the rest of your body—or anybody else—to keep up with your thoughts?

Do you feel like the parental figure of your friend group, the one who takes responsibility for the safety and well-being of your friends and loved ones more often than not?

Do you feel like you simply have too much information flowing through your brain, and you just have to get it out to somebody who understands your line of thinking the way that you do?

Do you feel like in any situation where you faced hardship, you would be able to easily and efficiently adapt to that situation and change gears to meet the new obstacles that the situation faced you with?

Are you a fan of conspiracy theories, even theories that everyone else might consider too obscure to be feasible? Do you relish in exploring these theories, in part because they are so outlandish to everyone else?

Do you feel like many of your efforts for others go unnoticed or less acknowledged than you would like, or what you're someone who deserves more praise and recognition?

Do people make note of your versatility, either in the workplace or in more public/personal groups?

Are you the type to go out of your way to give so much to people that they're obligated to give you something in return, or praise you?

Do your friends and family sometimes describe you as being too temperamental, or emotionally unstable on bad days?

Do you feel anxious that the friends you have now might turn their backs on you if you don't keep engaging them as normal?

Do you pride yourself on being able to "wing it", using your personality and optimistic attitude to get you out of a potentially negative or even dangerous situation?

Is it commonplace for you to be told you're brutally honest, or that you're way too combative?

Are you afraid of conflict within a professional or friend group, even if you're not involved directly in that conflict in any way?

Is it common for people to tell you that you're too high-strung around other people, or that you're paranoid of them to the point of antisocial behavior?

Once you've answered all of the questions to your satisfaction, go through them once again to answer them more honestly if you felt that your initial instinct may not have been the most accurate response. After all initial changes, please refrain from editing your answers anymore, except for instances where you would like to take the entire test again.

Chapter 13: The First Personality

In the scale of the nine personalities, the first one has different names such as the idealist, the reformer, the perfectionist, the purpose-driven, the principled, and the self-controlled. This might be because of the context of usage. The critical thing to remember is that they all mean the same thing. The term to be used in this chapter is that of the reformer. They are given these names because of their love of making anything they are involved in better. They are perfectionists who strive to make order out of everything regardless of how chaotic. They strive to be perfect, and when unable to be that, they do their best to try and strike a balance. This is because they love being remembered for good deeds.

The Description of the Reformer

The reformer loves to be viewed as without faults and is very good at keeping their morals in check. The bearer of this personality has good ethics. As well as a high priority for doing the right things and differentiating the wrong. They always try with utmost carefulness to avoid mistakes in order for people not to scold them or be disappointed. People with this personality are very noble, wise, and realistic in every situation.

They could be regarded as people-pleasers —always wanting to be right in the sight of others. Though they have the problem of inadequate patience while doing things, their comportment and maintenance of excellence, high standards and orderliness are part of what makes them unique. People who fall into this category are always orderly and organized, and dislike anyone that is less organized and thus are tagged perfectionists. In short, everything must be perfect for them no matter the situation.

Reformers put in a lot time correcting people which in turn, is why they detest being corrected themselves. The majority of the time, they avoid and complain about people that lag in their responsibilities, often they will be the ones to actually take note of this the fastest. Because they always love to shape the world around them to suit their needs and desires, they are often seen as social reformers. Reformers also tend to have a keen eye for detail and can notice when things are wrong, out of place, or not in a situation of perfection.

A fascinating fact about this personality type, perhaps true of others too, is that they have what drives them to behave and react this way —having a fear of being remembered for wrong deeds. They are always scared of doing wrong because they have infallible trust and integrity, appear to be accurate in all things, and so on. Everything and anything can motivate them. They are pushed by their desire to be the best among people, have a feeling of no guilt, improve in everything they do, and avoiding correction from people.

They're teachers at every point. Their ideals push them around with sincerity and strength. Funny enough, no matter how they grow, they love to accommodate people's view about things and admittance of the imperfectness in them. The motto of a reformer is "change what can be changed, about those that can't be changed, develop wisdom and tricks to know the difference between these things." They can be very resentful, however, whenever they get angry. They always know that "I am a responsible and objective person" –they barely deviate from this.

There are some things that reformers are used to, as well as a number of things that they can often be found doing. Below are some of the things they are well known for:

Cleanliness and order

Their surroundings have to be spotless and well arranged. When they are not reformers are generally uncomfortable and uneasy. Most of the time, when things are not done in accordance with how they would prefer those who fall into this personality group start to criticize. In order to affirm the existence of Enneagram, many scholars have given examples of each personality. Notable examples of reformers are Noam Chomsky, Confucius, Osama bin Laden, Celine Dion, Hillary Clinton, Plato George F. Will, Justice Sandra Day O'Connor, Nelson Mandela, etc.Some, although uncommon, have a mixture of reformer personality –it might not be the full one.

•They hate lies and dishonesty

If there is one thing that reformers truly detest it is liars and dishonest people. As much as a reformer tends to behave as a perfectionist in all things, they still won't stoop low to indulge themselves in dishonest dealings. This might even make a reformer break total ties with you completely.

•They always want to do things their own way

This is one of the attributes that makes them a perfectionist. A perfectionist will never bend nor will they sway from their beliefs, opinion, and ideas no matter how wrong they might turn out to be. They simply want things to be done in their own way. All perfectionists want to be head of a campaign or crusade no matter how shrewd it may seem. They just want to take the lead in anything they do. And no matter how wrong they might seem, other people's opinion doesn't really matter to them so long they end up achieving their own objective.

How to improve as a reformer

• Be patient

It is not uncommon for reformers who feel that they have done their best to better the people around them to realize that those people remain unmoved or unchanged. Often leaving the reformers to feel discouraged. When this happens, the best thing you can do is to exercise some patience. That you have done your very best, but ultimately cannot control another person's actions. It is more relieving and better not to be perfect at everything as there is always going to be a way around things.

Give them time to acculturate those things you want them to do —time heals all things. Your good deed will surely pay off in the lives of others. You're always a teacher; expecting behavioral changes in your 'students' will be an utmost concern to you, but in the end, always be patient.

• Reduce your harshness

Because you don't want people to see your faults, you get harder on yourself. Sometimes, you find yourself worrying over little things, especially after you've done something wrong and harmful to others around you. Don't punish yourself too much; you are human, after all. The way you'd do to others you see in the 'wrong' acts is what you do on yourself. The self-irritations you develop can barely solve the problem, and being friendly with people makes things easier. Understand yourself by considering those things that irritate you and device a better approach to dealing with them, so they do not get to you as much.

• Make sure you have enough time to relax

As much as reformers tend to always be on the go, it is crucial to know that the body needs rest too. Sometimes, reformers tend to go overboard in satisfying the need of everyone around them no matter the consequences. Additionally, they also put in more effort into making sure things go in order even if it means over stressing the body to achieve it. We should know that our body needs to rest in order to function well. Thus, keep your body fresh and healthy at all times. That is the only way you can achieve everything that you have planned.

• Know you are human too

Even if you fall into the reformer category - you are not a robot. It would do you a lot of good if you can keep this in mind at all times. No matter how hard you try to control your emotions, you would still come to terms with the fact that we cannot control our feelings. If at all, we can manage it, then it is only the outcome of our emotions that we can take control of. Additionally, we should also have it at the back of our mind that no matter how hard we try to be perfect, there are still going to be traces of imperfection around us. Don't feel bad when this happens. Don't get down on yourself when you start experiencing these kinds of errors in your perfect life. Don't let it weigh you down. In conclusion, reformers strive to do the right things. It is a compulsion they feel from the core of their being. They love everybody to have a high opinion of themselves, even though this is impossible. The reformers are perfectionists, and as such, they always want to be perfect in everything they do. This is the life of a reformer explained.

Now ask yourself if this is where you belong. Ask yourself if this particular personality fits your description. And if it does, then you should follow the various ways we listed above, on improving yourself. That is the only way you will be able to adjust with other personality types. But if you don't quite fit this personality type, don't worry. There are still eight more personality types, as you will see you in the next chapter

Chapter 14: The Enneagram As A New

Guide To Life

Every new chapter and every new discover in your life will offer you with the advice and the help that we all need in order to find ourselves and to make some kind of sense of the world that we live in. None of us are able to do this entirely on our own. Nor should we. After all, this is why there are so many people in the world from so many different cultures and walks of life, who will help to guide you to a new path and a new destination in achieving your dreams and helping people to achieve theirs.

Remarkably, the Enneagram is one of the most important discoveries pertaining the human psychology hat is currently available. It goes back many years into our past and has been analyzed and researched by thousands of people. Although some have found slight disagreements with others, the thing that we can all agree on is that the symbols of the Enneagram is indeed a very accurate representation of human personality, how it forms, how it functions, and how it can be steered towards a more positive side.

In the past couple of decades, the Enneagram has become a staple in school, workplaces, politics, universities and even medicine. The more we are able to discover about the human mind, the more we will look for ways to deal with our own problems effectively, without losing our cool and without doing things which we may later regret.

Whenever you find yourself in a situation where you feel like you need a sort of guidance in making a decision or deciding how you should feel about something, it is always a good idea to draw an Enneagram and to mark the position where you are currently finding yourself at the moment. By doing this, you can predict where your next level of personality shift will come (remember the lines that connect all of the levels?) and you can also tell which section of the intelligence level you are currently in. all of this information is enough to provide you with an objective view of where you can expect to find yourself at the moment in life. This is an excellent way to determine things because you don't have to worry about whether or not other people are telling you the truth when you ask them for advice about what you should do. Remember, the Enneagram does not have feelings. It only has the instructions that you need to live a better life and to make you a better person.

Learning About the Enneagram Is A Continuous Process

You cannot simply go through the journey of the Enneagram once and think that you have everything figured out. There are so many different layers to this view of the human personality that it really takes a few years to truly master it and to remember every aspect of it. But this is a good thing. Every time you go through this process, you will have a better understanding of who you are as a person and how you can improve. You will also have a better understanding of how other people around you function and what are the things that could make them spiral in either a positive or a negative direction. There may not be an entirely correct or incorrect answer to any of this, but remember that the point is to keep exploring and keep learning how to recognize the triggers that might make you turn into someone who you really don't want to become.

And if you really want to make the most of the Enneagram, use it to help other people discover themselves and their true purpose. Share your knowledge about the Enneagram symbol with others, and watch as they begin to form new opinions about the world and how they can help to make it a better place. And remember, if you notice that someone is behaving in a way that you don't like or that looks dangerous, it is because their personalities and their instincts have not aligned properly. Instead of immediately judging them for their behavior, why not do something what will help them to understand why they are behaving this way and how they can lead a better path in life?

Chapter 15: Enneagram For Relationship

Both Enneagram Twos and Sixes are particularly dutiful and take their duties very seriously. The emphasis is slightly different, however, with Twos specifically focused on building intimacy and positive feelings between himself and various individuals, while the emphasis of Sixes tends to be on the basis of safety, a strong platform for hard work. And believe that each person can depend. Both types are surprisingly accountable and have a tendency to put the desires of others ahead of themselves. They are each domestic-oriented and foster domestic; They share responsibilities around the house and with their youth or friends without difficulty. They are both socially concerned in their community and see extraordinary value in having many social relationships that make them realize that they are valued in their world. The sixes value warmth, kindness, generosity, and self-sacrifice of two. The sixes are aware of how well-suited dosas are to excellent, devoted spouses and parents, and that they can be trusted to be loyal.

On the other hand, the Twos will likely praise hard work, perseverance for commitments, perseverance, humility and the versatility of sixes. Even if they become grumpy and malleable now and again, Twos assumes that almost sixes come to an almost continuous end. Caution and vigilance are diagnosed as rewarding possessions in a cruel and exploitative world. Twice often it is understandable that they can be counted on monitoring six to see difficulties before they emerge as problems. When the Twos and Sixes are healthy, they can honestly admire each other more than they feel for each other in a grand arch. Their relationship may be based more on continuity, mutual respect, and affection than any kind of overheated chemistry between them. They see fractions as excellent and reliable, and this is more than enough as a basis for a regular, sustainable and productive lifestyle.

Potential trouble location or issue

One of the major viable areas for the troubles between Twos and Sixes has to do with management and autonomy, with a long way to go in addition to too much closure. Part of the problem has to do with working sixes' lack of self-confidence and decision-making ability and being decisive. Average sixes have a sense of coercion through all kinds of competing demands on their time and energy - by two, through bosses, my friends, through their church, and even by their country. Pressure from all aspects makes the sixes more anxious and emotionally unstable, not really feeling like it or unable to make easy decisions. They can be suspicious, suspicious and negative. As sixes are more reactive, they make every effort to take any action to overcome their anxiety moment by moment. At such times, Twos may also begin to give them additional help and advice or assist "orders" to empower the Sixes and help them overcome their anxiety.

However, the Sixers generally seek the two's help as they try and lower their self-confidence, and they resent it. After the cycle of rashness and outward appearances, with the aid of a tear-filled reunion, was observed with the need to become more and more independent on the part of Six, observed through additional intrusion on part two, spoiling this relationship Can. The problem is that twos with lower functioning believe that there is no such aspect as too much intimacy on the grounds that they are usually chosen closer. However, the sixes are extra bisexual, pushing both of them away and then pulling them closer. Six's ambition and inconsistency drive the two crazy and faucets out of fear of rejection. Twos wakes up once attempting to help six more people, even though the sixes travel as help to control them, and they are looking for more distance. The pair may be overwhelmed into a sinister child, embellishing parental drama that could ultimately be fatal to their relationship and the genuine mutual respect it was focused on with suspicion.

Chapter 16: Subtypes In The Enneagram

About The 27 Subtypes

As with most personality typing systems, the Enneagram can sometimes feel incomplete if you try to view yourself as just one whole Enneatype. The development of subtypes within each Enneatype help you to understand your personality type and where you are at in your evolution at a far deeper level. We are not just a single Enneatype. AT any given time, we can travel up and down our evolutionary ladder around the circle based on times of stress or security.

Subtypes of each Enneatype are broken into three basics for understanding. We have those aspects of our selves that show us how we deal with self-preservation, social situations, and one-to-one relationships, which can also include our sexual nature. These subtypes can be considered our most basic instincts for survival in each category. It is how we instinctively react in these situations, without thought.

We each have these subtypes within our personality Enneatype; however, these usually develop naturally, in a different priority level for each of us. The subtype we can most readily identify within our Enneatype is often what is considered to be our dominant subtype, the second would be our secondary, while the third is often found to be our repressed subtype.

These subtypes can also be viewed with an eye of where we go when we stress or succeed, our Disintegration and Integration points. By knowing where we go to at an instinctual level, we can begin to develop and evolve ourselves into healthier, more balanced individuals, and strengthen our relationships with the rest of the world.

Ones: The Perfectionist

Self-Preservation Ones: The Pioneer

Self-Preservation Ones can be very warm and friendly, but they are also the most worried and anxious types of the Enneagram. Their focus is on perfectionism and will work hard to make everything perfect. This focus on work is often used to cover the anxiety they have for always feeling they, themselves, are less than perfect. They want to impose order on all that is around them for what they feel is always doing the right thing.

Social Ones: The Social Reformer

When on their own home court, the Social Reformer Ones are very outgoing and friendly. They have a hard time adapting to things not done in ways that they feel are the "right way," and can be both critical and resentful of others not following their perceived set of proprietary rules. These Ones can be good teachers, and they see themselves in that role, always trying to teach others their image of perfect. They are often socially correct, but their hindrance lies in their inability to change and adapt.

One-To-One Ones: The Evangelist

The One-to-One Ones have a zealousness unmatched by other Enneatypes or subtypes. Where Ones tend to focus on making themselves perfect, these Ones have a focus more on bringing others, and the rest of society, to a state of perfection. They pay a great deal of attention to whether they perceive others as doing, or not doing things right, according to their own very strict standards. They also have a deep jealous nature, not only for those they love or are partners with but also for those who may have a greater amount of self-expression.

Twos: The Giver

Self-Preservation Twos: The Nurturer

Self-Preservation Twos are very nurturing and connect with many different people on many levels, although they tend to be a little more afraid about making those connections than other Twos. The side of their nurturing, however, can come at a cost to those they care for. Their nurturing takes on a form of entitlement for care in getting their own needs met. In actuality, their charm is turned on in a nurturing style without conscious awareness that their true motives are to be taken care of as a result.

Social Twos: The Ambassador

Social Twos play to the recognition of their accomplishments and like to prove their value by stepping in and taking charge. They take on what they can to make themselves invaluable to others, using their ambition to gain recognition and self-esteem. Although being on center stage for these individuals is not always as important to them as making the right connections to further their ambitions.

One-To-One Twos: The Lover

One-to-One Twos can have two distinct sides, one of either aggression or the use of seduction to gain attention and recognition in personal relationships and interactions. They strive to be generous and make themselves attractive to win the approval of their selected target, even if they plan on making it a short-term goal or relationship. Their tone is often seductive, although not necessarily of a sexual nature. The One-to-One Two can be more passionate and emotional than others Twos and has no problem bringing attention to their appealability and promises of support to win the attraction and approval of others.

Threes: The Performer

Self-Preservation Threes: The Company Man/Woman

Self-Preservation Threes tend to immerse themselves into work and whatever else it may take to achieve material success and security for themselves and anyone around them. They are all about image, although they don't like tooting their own horn, because they don't feel that is a good image to project. They like to look good and show themselves as "good" to the social spectrum they are connected to. They are results-oriented people who work hard and prove themselves to be very self-sufficient.

Social Threes: The Politician

Social Threes know instinctively how to climb the social ladder, and do so in order to achieve the material and other status symbols that society views as markers of having the right "image." These Threes can be true social leaders, or they may just have the ability for hype and propaganda, forcing others to see the image they want to be projected. Prestige and social success are the epitomes of being in the winners' circle for this highly competitive subtype.

One-To-One Threes: The Movie Star

One-to-One Threes are less focused on their own personal successes, as they are on supporting the successes of their partners and others around them. The success of their image comes with a focus on either femininity or masculinity, and how well they are perceived as such. They have strong ties to gender issues and identity, although they may have some confusion when it comes to their own contemplation of these same issues. They are very strong team players with powerful charisma.

Fours: The Romantic

Self-Preservation Fours: The Creative Individualist

Self-Preservation Fours search for authenticity in everything around them and will go at great lengths to find it, even to the point of being reckless. These unorthodox creative types have no problem throwing caution to the wind and just picking up and jumping into a new place or situation if they feel the need for self-preservation. They may appear stoic on the outside, but inside they can be highly emotionally sensitive. Their feelings and emotions can run dark, and they are afraid to share that side of themselves with others. Their tolerance for frustration is high, and even though they may stress to feelings of anxiety or sadness, they try to tough things out and put on a happy face to the world.

Social Fours: The Critical Commentator

Social Fours focus on the intensity and authenticity of their own emotions versus societal expectations. They are highly critical of themselves, and when they compare themselves to others, they usually feel that they are lacking or not worthy in some way or another. This deficiency is often felt when in social situations, and they tend toward feelings of enviousness at the easier way that others seem to fit in, or seem to belong. They have strong inclinations in the validity of their emotions, and may sometimes wear their heart on their sleeve.

One-To-One Fours: The Dramatic Person

One-to-One Fours are highly competitive and take the strengths of others as a personal challenge to come out on top in any situation. If they do not feel stronger than the other person, more accomplished, falling short on a tally of achievements, their personal value suffers. One-to-One Fours can sometimes come off as aggressive, and will always list their achievements as being better than another's. They will use power or style to beat the competition and to create within themselves the ability to move forward with their own personal agenda.

Fives: The Observer

Self-Preservation Fives: The Castle Defender

Self-Preservation Fives can be of one of two types. They can either use their home as their personal castle or fortress—a place where they retreat to with feelings of safety. Or, they may forego having an attachment to any single place and spend their time moving around or traveling. Even so, there is a need for either type to have a private space for alone time when they feel the need. Self-Preservation Fives can be very friendly and have a genuine warmth. They like to keep their needs minimal and have all that they may need or want at any time within the safety of their private haven.

Social Fives: The Professor

Social Fives thrive on acquiring knowledge and work hard to become experts in the fields or areas that they find of interest. They very much enjoy connecting with those who may share the same causes they believe in, or have common ground in their intellectual interests. This may lead to them having stronger connections with these people, then they may have with those they have around them as family, friends, or otherwise. Their ability to participate with others in a given situation can be hindered by their tendency to over-think, over-analyze, and observe, offering their knowledge as a form of teaching that often comes from study as opposed to experience.

One-To-One Fives: The Secret Agent

One-to-One Fives can be inwardly more emotionally connected or aware than any other aspect of the Five Enneatype. This still doesn't usually mean they show it outwardly but tend to only share that secretive side of themselves in an intimate setting. While they struggle with a preference to maintain autonomy, they also want to share that secret, emotional side of themselves with another being with whom they feel an intimate emotional connection. These Five types can have a flair for the romantic that may demonstrate itself in some form of artistic or creative expression.

Sixes: The Loyal Skeptic

Self-Preservation Sixes: The Family Loyalist

Self-Preservation Sixes tend toward more of the flight side of the fight or flight spectrum. They constantly question and doubt things and circumstances to try and find a sense of comfort and certainty to feel safer and secure in any given situation. They look to others outside themselves for protection and work in a friendly manner with affection and warmth to attract those they would see as protective allies.

Social Sixes: The Social Guardian

Social Sixes have a need for clarity about their role in society or even in a group. They need clear boundaries and rules set for social interaction, because they fear rejection, and have the need to know how to avoid it. They have a strong sense of duty and will live up to it, although depending on the situation, it can either feel like a calling or a burden. Social Sixes are far more logical and rational than Self-Preservation Sixes, which helps them to be certain and confident. They like to focus on making benchmarks, and finding reference points to ensure they live up to the protection from the outside sources that they feel they need.

One-To-One Sixes: The Warrior

Where Self-Preservation Sixes lean toward the flight side of the fight or flight spectrum, One-to-One Sixes jump to the fight side of the equation. The saying that the best defense is a good offense is very applicable to One-to-One Sixes, and they quickly leap to defend their ideologies and idealism fiercely. This can easily turn them into the role of risk-takers or rebels, and they use their contrary nature to create control and stability in their lives to deal with their underlying fears, even though they may not be aware that these fears exist.

Sevens: The Epicure

Self-Preservation Sevens: The Gourmand

Self-Preservation Sevens enjoy good conversation, spending quality family time, planning and implementing fun projects and dining out or sharing elaborately prepared food with others. They are more hedonistic than most other Enneatypes or subtypes and can lean toward over-stimulation in their quest for enjoyment. Their lifestyle leans toward one of abundance, and they enjoy sharing it with others. They have an instinctive knowledge of how to make things happen, which makes them regularly successful at getting and achieving what they want from life.

Social Sevens: The Utopian Visionary

The Seven Enneatype is a planner who does not like putting limitations on the expansion of their own personal awareness and achievements, so the Social Seven is quite the dichotomy, with their need for expression of the love of life and their social ideals through others, such as groups and friends. They do not want to appear that the only interests they have are their own or that they are opportunistic. Social Sevens dedicate themselves in service to others around them as a way of pushing aside their own personal desires in the present. They prefer to show themselves to the world as those who would ease the suffering of others.

One-To-One Sevens: The Adventurer

One-to-One Sevens are optimistically enthusiastic dreamers with a passionate need to see things as they would want or imagine them to be as opposed to the reality that is truly before them. They jump right on board with a fascinated attraction to a new adventure, but this fascination also carries weight with new people or new ideas that come across their path. One-to-One Sevens are highly suggestible and easily excited. However, they can just as easily raise the suggestibility levels in others with their personal charm.

Eights: The Protector

Self-Preservation Eights: The Survivalist

Self-Preservation Eights are far more suited to a hostile world than a friendly one. Their focus is on whatever it is that they feel needed to survive. They fight to win, especially when it comes to protecting themselves, personal space, or family, and will go down fighting to achieve that win, if necessary. They are not the types to give in! Self-Preservation Eights get frustrated easily, especially when they feel what they want or want to achieve is not happening in a timely enough fashion.

Social Eights: The Group Leader/Gang Leader

The often-rebellious Social Eights are leaders who are fierce and loyally committed to their preference for social causes and friends. The usual aggression, often fueled by anger, found in the Eight Enneatype is softened by their need to care for others, and will harness their aggression to lead their group toward a common goal or agenda. To those that they feel are in need of support, they are protective mentor types and will move the feelings and needs of others to a higher place on their priority list than their own.

One-To-One Eights: The Commander

Also in possession of an often-rebellious nature, One-to-One Eights find preference in being right at the center of whatever is going on. This subtype has a strong tendency toward possession for the sake of control and can prove quite forceful about it, even (or especially) when this applies to a personal partner. They enjoy the power they can hold over the various situations and people they encounter. Their true drive is for surrender, and seek that special someone to whom they would find themselves comfortable enough with to just let go and surrender.

Nines: The Mediator

Self-Preservation Nines: The Collector

Self-Preservation Nines have an appetite for material consumption, and whether this is food or just "things," they can find themselves doing and/or collecting anything that will take their focus away from their own personal needs. Familiar routines and daily rhythms guide the comfort levels of Self-Preservation Nines, and they like to ground themselves by losing themselves in whatever activity will keep them otherwise preoccupied.

Social Nines: The Community Benefactor

Social Nines seek comfort and belonging in social circles and groups. Their light-hearted and fun style tends to blend well with others, and Social Nines will do whatever they can, and whatever it takes to prove themselves invaluable for their admittance to being part of the group. This subtype can show themselves to be great leaders, willing to work for the common agenda of the group toward good. They still have the tendency, like most Nine types, to forget any focus on personal priorities and/or needs.

One-To-One Nines: The Seeker

One-to-One Nines have a focus on merging with something or someone outside of themselves, including nature as a possibility of reaching a more transcendent state. These Nines are relationship-oriented and sweet-natured. They do lack an assertiveness when it comes to self and have a hard time maintaining personal boundaries and a sense of individual self. They can easily find themselves taking on or adapting to the opinions and feelings of those who are important and close to them.

Chapter 17: Enneagram Type 3

In this section, you will see eight good qualities, eight stressors, and eight stress behaviors of Enneagram Type 3.

Mark with a tick which ones apply to you.

GOOD QUALITIES

3s are productive individuals. They have a gift for finding a more effective way to do things. 3s work hard and enjoy producing a lot in a short space of time.

3s are accomplished. They apply themselves tirelessly to their work and often rise to positions of leadership. Being in this position allows them to achieve more and accomplish more. 3s work hard to make the world a better place. And you can always count on a 3 to deliver as they move towards making their dream a reality.

3s make efficient use of their time and they are always on the move. They are the ones who are often multi-tasking and

doing many things at the same time. Typing while walking, replying to an email while having breakfast, 3s make the most out of every minute of time. They are normally multi-tasking with an abundance of various activities all going on at the same time.

3s have a laser-like focus. They can hone in on whatever needs to be done, then they can focus all their energy on bringing it to pass. Many leaders and CEOs are 3s. With so many things to be done as the leader of the company, a 3 will help focus the energy of the group and guide the rest of the employees, showing them the way to go. In a boardroom, 3s would focus on directly hashing out all the issues. After the meeting, the work can then be delegated so that everyone knows what they are doing.

3s are competent individuals. In their chosen field they find out everything they can and becoming the best they can be. They are capable people who are always

learning, and improving themselves. 3s take what they learn and immediately put it into action, and they are not afraid to experiment with new ways of doing things in order to find a better way. They appear confident, and through trial and error eventually, they find the method that works best.

3s are driven, seeking to be the best in their field, not just in business, but in the sporting arena as well. Not all top athletes are 3s but many are, and they put thousands of hours of work into being the best in their field. They enjoy competing at the highest level and pushing the limits of what can be accomplished by a human being whether it is running the 100m sprint in under 10s, slam-dunking the ball, or winning major championships. The 3s are driving hard and working hard, and are often successful in whatever they set out to do.

3s are the center of the heart center. They are said to have the biggest heart of all.

They often use their success, wealth, and accomplishments and share it with their loved ones, friends, and society as a whole. Whether in the form of gifts, charity auctions, or setting up foundations for the poor, sick, and needy; you can find 3s involved in all kinds of ways of giving back.

3s are also inspiring in terms of demonstrating to others what is possible. They share their wisdom, experience, and accomplishments by inspiring younger kids and the underprivileged. 3s will teach them what they know, and how to do things better, and engage in activities such as mentoring and coaching the younger generations in areas such as business and sport.

STRESSORS

3s are overburdened by the sheer number of tasks to be done and having to continuously perform at the highest level. 3s believe if they do not produce or perform they will not be loved. Their heart is their center of intelligence and all information is interpreted through their heart. Like with the other heart types, they are also emotionally in tune with the feelings of the room. When the world of a 3 is not as it should be here are some of the thoughts and beliefs that can pop into their heads.

Conclusion

Thank you again for purchasing this book!

I hope this book was able to help you to understand your Ennea-type and the Types of people in your life. I hope this knowledge allows you to grow, recognize your own potential, and overcome challenges that hold you back.

The next step is to act! I've provided suggestions and solutions to help you achieve the best version of yourself, depending on your Type. So now, all you have to do is find the solution that works for you and live a happier, fuller life.

I'm so glad you've made it to the end of this book, and I hope you've found some worth in it. If you would be so kind, I'd really appreciate it if you would leave a positive review and share your experience, so others might be able to find this book and start their learning.

Thank you and good luck!

9 781990 084508